Peter Osborne is Professor of Modern European Philosophy at Middlesex University, London and an editor of the journal *Radical Philosophy*. His books include *The Politics of Time*, *Philosophy in Cultural Theory* and *Conceptual Art*. He is the editor of the three-volume *Walter Benjamin: Critical Evaluations in Cultural Theory*.

WITHDRAWN

HOW TO READ

Available now

Forthcoming

HOW
TO
READ

MARX

PETER OSBORNE

Granta Books
London

Granta Publications, 2/3 Hanover Yard, Noel Road, London N1 8BE

First published in Great Britain by Granta Books, 2005

A CIP catalogue record for this book is
available from the British Library.

ISBN-13: 978-1-86207-771-3
ISBN-10: 1-86207-771-1

1 3 5 7 9 10 8 6 4 2

Typeset by M Rules

Printed and bound in Great Britain by
Bookmarque Limited, Croydon, Surrey

CONTENTS

SERIES EDITOR'S FOREWORD

How am I to read *How to Read*?

This series is based on a very simple, but novel idea. Most beginners' guides to great thinkers and writers offer either potted biography or condensed summaries of their major works, or perhaps even both. *How to Read*, by contrast, brings the reader face-to-face with the writing itself in the company of an expert guide. Its starting point is that in order to get close to what a writer is all about, you have to get close to the words they actually use and be shown how to read those words.

Every book in the series is in a way a masterclass in reading. Each author has selected ten or so short extracts from a writer's work and looks at them in detail as a way of revealing their central ideas and thereby opening doors onto a whole world of thought. Sometimes these extracts are arranged chronologically to give a sense of a thinker's development over time, sometimes not. The books are not merely compilations of a thinker's most famous passages, their 'greatest hits', but rather they offer a series of clues or keys that will enable readers to go on and make discoveries of their own. In addition to the texts and readings, each book provides a short biographical chronology and suggestions for further reading, Internet resources, and so on. The books in the *How to Read* series don't claim to tell you all you need to know about Freud, Nietzsche and Darwin, or indeed Shakespeare and the Marquis de Sade, but they do offer the best starting point for further exploration.

Unlike the available second-hand versions of the minds that have shaped our intellectual, cultural, religious, political and scientific landscape, *How to Read* offers a refreshing set of first-hand encounters with those minds. Our hope is that these books will, by turns, instruct, intrigue, embolden, encourage and delight.

Simon Critchley
New School for Social Research, New York

ACKNOWLEDGEMENTS

Thanks to Simon Critchley and George Miller for the opportunity to write this book. I am grateful to John Kraniauskas and Stella Sandford for their comments on drafts, and to Stella for so much more as well. Thanks also to Bella Shand for her editorial work on the manuscript.

For Ilya

INTRODUCTION

> ... as there is no such thing as an innocent reading, we
> must say what reading we are guilty of.
>
> Louis Althusser, *Reading Capital*

This book is guilty of reading Marx philosophically. But before I explain what I mean by that, let me say why, at the beginning of the twenty-first century, I believe we should be reading Marx at all.

Marx is *the* thinker of nineteenth-century European capitalism – a giant among the great white males of late Enlightenment bourgeois culture. He was born in 1818 in Trier, in Prussia's Rhine Province, into the uncertainties of the post-Napoleonic era. He died in 1883, in the early stages of the imperialist rivalry between European powers that would culminate in the First World War. From the beginning of the 1840s until his death, Marx subjected the capitalist societies of Europe and beyond to the most profound analysis and scathing criticism they have ever received. In the phrase of the French philosopher Paul Ricoeur, he was one of the three great 'masters of suspicion', along with Nietzsche and Freud. Marx and Engels's *Manifesto of the Communist Party* (1848) is probably the most influential text ever written, outside of the great world religions.

But Marx was not simply a thinker of nineteenth-century European capitalism. He was a thinker of capitalism in itself. Marx was a thinker of the fundamental elements of capitalism as an economic system – the commodity, money, capital, labour, surplus value, accumulation and crisis – of their relations to each other, and their forms of development. He was the thinker of capitalism's basic tendency to universalize itself – to spread across the globe. He understood economic 'value' as a mysterious, alien, increasingly pervasive and all-engulfing social form, and he understood social labour as the source of human productivity, creativity, possibility and freedom. Marx's central thought is of humans as natural, social, practical and historical beings, and of history as an on-going struggle between classes. His view of capitalism is that it is constantly developing within the limits of its basic form, and that it can ultimately be no more than 'a passing histori-cal phase' of human production. Most important of all, Marx conceived an alternative future, contained within yet radi-cally moving beyond the capitalist present. 'The social revolution of the nineteenth century', he wrote in *The Eighteenth Brumaire of Louis Bonaparte* (1852), 'can only create its poetry from the future, not the past.' In this respect at least, the social revolutions of the twenty-first century will be no different.

It was fashionable, briefly, in the 1960s and 1970s, to speak of 'late capitalism', as if the historical period ushered in by the agricultural and industrial revolutions of the seventeenth and eighteenth centuries in Europe was nearing its end. The phrase carries with it a bitter irony today. With the collapse of 'actually existing socialism' (as it was called at the time) or his-torical communism (as it is called now) in Eastern Europe, the integration of the ex-colonial societies of the European empires into the circuits of global capital (via the creation of debt), and the wildfire of state-capitalism in China, it is more likely that we are in the later stages of 'early capitalism'. Many have assumed that the collapse of international communism consigned Marx's writings to a merely archival significance. Yet Marx was never the theorist of 'actually existing' state socialism, or of national liberation. That was the task of Lenin, Stalin, Trotsky, Mao and Guevara. Marx was – and remains – first and foremost a critical analyst of capitalism, a theorist of its social dynamics and the conditions needed to overcome it. With the spread of capitalism across the globe and its burgeoning in once 'under-developed' economies such as Brazil and India, Marx's writings have become more, not less relevant to the present. In particular, as what began in the early 1990s as the 'anti-globalization' movement becomes more self-consciously 'anti-capitalist' (at least in its rhetoric), it is increasingly important to know precisely what capitalism is. What distinguishes the concept of capitalism from the notion of a 'market society'? What does it mean to be subjected to value? What developmental tendencies are inherent within the social form of capital itself?

The passing of state socialism heralds the possibility of a new life for Marx's texts in another sense too: a life of interpretation freed from the political authority of orthodoxy where Marx's writings were codified into an educational system appropriate for party-political purposes. This orthodoxy was derived from the later writings of Marx's collaborator of forty years, Friedrich Engels (1820–95). It was developed in the USSR and disseminated from there, as 'Marxism-Leninism', within the world communist movement.

Reading is an established way of challenging orthodoxies. Codification requires interpretations that will never be intellectually adequate to the subtleties and contradictions of the texts on which it grounds its authority. The idea of reading, reading as interpretation, reading *against orthodoxy*, has played a central role in Enlightenment movements for the reform of education, at least since Martin Luther. Canonical texts provide a stage for conflicts between generations. In this respect, reading has enjoyed a special place in theoretical disciplines in the humanities since the libertarian movements of the 1960s. Marx's texts have been no exception; indeed, they have been exemplary.

The most productive readings of Marx in the Western tradition are those of Georg Lukács, Antonio Gramsci and Walter Benjamin in the 1920s and 1930s, Max Horkheimer and Theodor W. Adorno in the 1940s, and Louis Althusser in the 1960s. They are all heretical readings that use the letter of Marx's writings to squirm out of the straightjacket of orthodox interpretations. Each exploits the intellectual depth and richness of association of Marx's writing against established orthodoxies, readings that had become taken for granted. Yet none are content merely to point to a proliferation of meanings; none are content merely to dissent. Each uses its own historical position and set of problems to forge a new coherence, to project a new reading of the whole, a new thought.

This book reads Marx in the wake of those interpretations. Like them, it reads Marx both philosophically and from the standpoint of its own historical present. But this claim is in danger of being misunderstood. What I mean by a philosophical reading is a far cry from the prevailing sense of 'philosophy' in the English-speaking world, as a university discipline with its own largely formal, logical and linguistic subject matter. Marx himself was a notorious critic of philosophy in its academic, disciplinary sense. Philosophers, he wrote in the last of his theses 'On Feuerbach' (1845), are those who have 'only *interpreted* the world', when 'the point is to *change* it'. In *The German Ideology* (1845–6) we are told: 'Philosophy and the study of the real world have the same relation to one another as onanism and sexual love.' And perhaps most shocking, because most brutally reductive, in the same text: 'Every profound philosophical problem may be resolved quite simply into an empirical fact.'

However, this is a good example of the rhetorical strategy that Lenin dubbed 'bending the stick' in the opposite direction to which it is currently pointing, in order to straighten it out. What Marx meant by 'philosophy' in these passages was a purportedly rationally 'self-sufficient' discourse or mode of inquiry. Because of its presumption that reason could exist on its own, such a discourse is inherently idealist in character. But once the illusion of self-sufficiency has been dispelled, Marx argued, the field opens up for an alternative, *dependent* conception of philosophical thought, which Marx himself described in terms of 'a summing-up', a totalization of 'the most general results' of inquiries based on experience and observation. And it is here, he acknowledged, that 'the difficulties begin'. In this more difficult, dependent sense, philosophical discourse operates across disciplinary divisions at the level of their ultimate interconnections. It seeks out universal significance in apparently 'non-philosophical' domains, such as politics and the economy. And it constructs new transdisciplinary concepts, such as commodity fetishism, practice, mode of production, and alienation (discussed in chapters 1–4, respectively). It is this broad understanding of philosophy as a critical transdisciplinary intellectual practice, derived from Marx's writings, which I use to read Marx himself here.

In his writing, Marx strove to connect theoretical abstractions to experience, since it is as elements of experience that, ultimately, abstractions acquire truth. Conceptual abstractions transfigure the experiences they relate to – much like novels and works of visual art transfigure the experience of their readers and viewers. These are the 'phenomenological' and 'existential' aspects of Marx's thought. Marx engages his readers via the way the world appears to them, then traces these appearances back to fundamental features of human existence, so as to demonstrate their ultimate practical significance. To read Marx philosophically is to recover this level of meaning and to connect it to one's own experience as a practical social being. It is here that the striking imagery of Marx's prose (and that of some of his translators) is of such importance: the literary form and the philosophical aspirations of Marx's writings are closely linked.

In selecting extracts I have been guided by a combination of motives: to convey the distinctiveness and depth of Marx's thought; to focus on passages that require and reward close reading, passages that are important but not readily understood; to treat Marx's analysis of capitalism as an integral part of his philosophical thought; to prioritize the analysis of capitalism over Marx's more immediately political writings, which have less current significance; to present Marx's views as an ongoing process of investigation, rather than a doctrine; and to highlight some of the pleasures and power of his prose, to the extent to which it can be carried over in translation.

Specialized terminology is often the greatest barrier for the general reader in approaching scientific and philosophical texts. Yet, as Engels put it in his preface to the first English edition of Marx's *Capital* (1888), this is 'one difficulty we could not spare the reader' since 'every new aspect of a science involves a revolution in the technical terms of that science'. Marx both invented his own technical terms in his critique of political economy and used the inherited philosophical vocabulary of German idealism. It is a distinctive feature of that tradition that it built a specialized terminology out of words that also have everyday meanings. This double coding of the language – both specialized and everyday – has been crucial to the cultural function of philosophy in European societies, mediating between the specialized languages of the academy and public discourse. To a large extent, to understand a thinker within this tradition simply is to come to terms with this dual use of language. Marx belongs to this tradition. In particular, in his published works, he was also writing for the workers' movement. Marx's prose is thus characteristically a delicious mix of theory and metaphor, technical abstruseness and political bluntness. To read Marx most productively is to read him at all these levels simultaneously.

A Note on Sources and Translation

Marx wrote mainly in German. I have used two English-language sources for citations from Marx's texts: Ben Fowkes's translation of *Capital*, volume 1, first published by Penguin in association with New Left Review, 1976, and the Marx/Engels *Collected Works*, published in fifty volumes by Lawrence and Wishart, 1975ff. The *Collected Works* includes Samuel Moore's wonderful 1888 translation of the *Communist Manifesto*, which is a work of literature in its own right. However, in some instances, the *Collected Works* (along with other published translations of the passages concerned) proves to be inadequate for the purposes of close reading, for two reasons. First, it is often insensitive to the now-established conventions for translating German philosophical terminology. Second, it follows outdated gender norms. Reading the still-standard translations of most of Marx's writings of the 1840s, one has the impression that the human species is made up exclusively of males. Where necessary I have retranslated extracts as a whole, using the Marx/Engels *Gesamtausgabe* first published by Dietz Verlag, Berlin, 1975ff. On occasion, I have simply altered the gendering of personal pronouns and certain inappropriately gendered phrases. Within the main text, references to *Capital*, Volume 1, appear in parentheses as *C* 1, followed by the page numbers of the Penguin edition; those to the English-language *Collected Works* appear as *MECW*, followed by the volume and page numbers.

1

COMMODITY: FETISH AND HIEROGLYPH

A commodity appears at first sight an obvious, trivial thing. But its analysis brings out that it is a very strange thing, abounding in metaphysical subtleties and theological niceties. So far as it is a use-value, there is nothing mysterious about it, whether we consider it from the point of view that by its properties it satisfies human needs, or that it first takes on these properties as the product of human labour. It is absolutely clear that, by its activity humanity changes the form of the materials of nature in such a way as to make them useful to it. The form of wood, for instance, is altered if a table is made out of it. Nevertheless the table continues to be wood, an ordinary, sensible thing. But as soon as it emerges as a commodity, it changes into a thing that transcends sensuousness. It not only stands with its feet on the ground, but, in relation to all other commodities, it stands on its head, and evolves out of its wooden brain grotesque ideas, far more wonderful than if it were to begin dancing of its own free will.

The mysterious character of the commodity does not therefore arise from its use-value. Just as little does it proceed from the content of the determinations of value . . .

Whence, then, arises the enigmatic character of the

product of labour, as soon as it assumes the form of a commodity? Clearly from this form itself . . .

The mysteriousness of the commodity-form consists . . . in the fact that the commodity reflects back the social characteristics of people's own labour as objective characteristics of the products of labour themselves, as social natural-properties of these things. Hence it also reflects the social relation of the producers to the totality of labour as a social relation between objects that exists outside of them. Through this substitution, this *quid pro quo*, the products of labour become commodities, sensuous things which are at the same time suprasensible or social . . . the commodity-form, and the value-relation of the products of labour within which it appears, have absolutely no connection with the physical nature of the commodity and the material relations arising out of this. It is nothing but the determinate social relation between people themselves that assumes here, for them, the fantastic [phantasmagorical] form of a relation between things. In order, therefore, to find an analogy we must take flight into the misty realm of the religious world. There the products of human brains appear endowed with a life of their own, self-sufficient figures entering into relations with each other and with humans. So it is in the commodity-world with the products of human hands. I call this the fetishism that attaches itself to the products of labour as soon as they are produced as commodities, and which is therefore inseparable from the production of commodities. . . .

Value, therefore, does not have its description branded on its forehead; it rather transforms every product of labour into a social hieroglyphic.

Extract from 'The Fetish Character of
the Commodity and its Secret', *Capital:
A Critique of Political Economy, Volume 1*, 2nd edn, 1873

Commodity fetishism is probably the best known of Marx's critical ideas about the capitalist economy. It is certainly the most immediately engaging idea in his complex and voluminous analysis of capitalism as a mode of production in his (unfinished) magnum opus, *Capital* – the published text of which runs to nearly 2000 pages. Most people are familiar with some notion of fetishism. However, the form of fetishism most commonly represented in capitalist cultures (in pornography, fashion magazines and advertisements) is sexual fetishism: the fixation of desire on a particular part of the body, type of object or material, such as feet, shoes, fur or rubber. A broadly Freudian, psycho-sexual conception of fetishism has thus come to prevail, in the culture of capitalism, with which Marx's notion of commodity fetishism is often confused.[1] (This is particularly the case in certain kinds of cultural studies.) There is a tendency to assume that Marx's commodity fetishism is also about the fixing of desire, but on a different kind of object, the commodity: an investment of desire in the ownership of commodities. But this is not what Marx's account of the fetish character of the commodity is about.

The clue lies in the title of the relevant section of *Capital*: 'The Fetish Character of the Commodity and its Secret'. Marx's account is not about fetishism as a psychological condition of a subject, whose desire transforms the significance of particular objects. It is about the fetish character of the commodity itself, a special kind of object: specifically, the fetish character of its 'form', the commodity-form. For Marx, the commodity-form is 'the value-form of the commodity', the commodity considered not as a physical entity, but as a value (*C* 1, 90). What Marx is referring to with the idea of commodity fetishism is thus not the fetishization of particular commodities by individual consumers. It is a 'fetishism that attaches itself to the products of labour as soon as they are produced *as* commodities'. It derives from the social relations of production and is a feature of the capitalist mode of production in general. (For Marx, capitalist societies are those in which commodity production based on wage-labour prevails.) What we might call consumer fetishism, on the other hand, is part of a historically much more particular regime of circulation of consumer goods to which advertising, design and display – a whole apparatus of 'commodity aesthetics' – is central. Marx's conception is both more general and involves a more socially fundamental explanation.

To understand Marx's idea of commodity fetishism, we need to be clear about two things. First, what is involved when something is 'produced as a commodity'? Second, what was at stake for Marx in the 'analogy' of fetishism? What was the context within which the term operated in mid-nineteenth-century Europe?

Marx considers commodity fetishism at the end of the first chapter of *Capital*, 'The Commodity', and his discussion depends upon the analysis that precedes it. To understand commodity fetishism, we must first familiarize ourselves with Marx's account of the commodity as the 'elementary form' of wealth in capitalist societies. Simple as the commodity might seem, this is the part of *Capital* that Marx acknowledged presents 'the greatest difficulty' to the reader (*C* 1, 89). Marx's analysis of the commodity is perhaps his greatest thought. He begins by pointing out that every commodity has both a 'use-value' and an 'exchange-value'. (This is why, far from being 'obvious' and 'trivial', a commodity can become a strange, tricky or mixed-up thing.) A use-value is a property that satisfies some human need, such that someone might want to purchase the commodity. An exchange-value is a quantitative measure of the value of a commodity in relation to other commodities. It is the possession of exchange-value that makes a product a commodity. To be produced as a commodity is to be produced *for exchange*. Commodity production is production for exchange.

Marx's analysis goes further by arguing that in commodity production, labour also has a two-fold or 'double' character. Marx calls these aspects 'concrete labour' and 'abstract labour', corresponding to labour's production of the use-value and exchange-value of commodities, respectively. 'Concrete labour' designates the particular skills and practices necessary to produce a particular kind of object: the sawing, planing and hammering necessary to produce a table from wood, for example. Abstract labour, on the other hand, refers to the expenditure of human labour-power in general, in the production of commodities. Marx argues that it is only when labour is reduced to this single homogeneous quality that concrete labours become measurably comparable, and their products can be exchanged for money. It is as the source of abstract labour that labour-power itself is commodified. The standpoint of abstract labour is the standpoint of exchange. Chronological time is Marx's unit of measure for abstract labour. In this account, the 'socially average' time taken to produce a commodity is the measure of its relationship to other commodities. This is Marx's labour theory of value, but it is not what concerns us here.

What concerns us is the effect of abstract labour on the social being of the commodity – on what it most fundamentally is. According to Marx, when labour-power is bought as a commodity, for wages, within a process of commodity production, it is the labourer's capacity to produce exchange-value, rather than use-value, that is being purchased. Use-values are produced too, of course, since nothing without a use-value can be exchanged, but in commodity production the real goal of the process is exchange-value. Use-values are merely its material bearers. More specifically, the goal is an exchange-value greater than that of the factors of production as a whole: a 'surplus' value. On sale, this surplus value is realized as profit. Such, in a nutshell, is Marx's economics of the commodity.

The reason a commodity is a 'mysterious' thing, according to Marx, is that its possession of exchange-value endows it with characteristics unrelated to either its use or its sensible, material form. When a product of labour emerges as a commodity, it is a 'sensuous' thing that is also at the same time 'suprasensible or social'. (Marx's original German is much more direct in expressing a contradiction here. He called it *ein sinnlich übersinnliches Ding*: literally, 'a sensible suprasensible thing'.) It has both sensibly perceptible qualities and sensibly imperceptible ones. For example, a table is 'an ordinary sensible thing' with a particular size and shape, made of a certain kind of wood. As an exchange-value, on the other hand, it expresses a quantitative relation between the abstract labour it embodies and the abstract labour embodied in other commodities. This has nothing to do with any of its sensible, perceptible, material features. Metaphysically speaking, exchange-value is thus *ideal*. Marx was quite explicit about this; earlier on in *Capital* he wrote: 'Not an atom of matter enters into the objectivity of commodities as values . . . their objectivity as values is purely social' (*C* 1, 138).

Moreover, Marx argues, this 'suprasensible' aspect, which is expressed through price, is the *only* way that the social side of the commodity appears; it is the only way 'private labour manifests itself as a member of the social total-labour' (*C* 1, 165). The concrete relationships of cooperation and dependency between different types of labour that are needed to produce commodities are invisible. They have no discernible social expression. Yet in practice they knit the very fabric of society. Furthermore, and this is Marx's critical point, the commodity's suprasensible property – exchange-value – appears *as if* it was an 'objective', 'socio-natural' property of the object itself. Value appears to be embedded in the product.

When we encounter a car, a computer or a washing machine we see its price as an expression of the value of the sensible object itself, rather than of the labour it embodies. We don't think about who produced and who assembled its components, or under what conditions. This is the sense in which a commodity 'reflects back the social characteristics of people's own labour as objective characteristics of the products of labour themselves'. Social relations between people assume 'the fantastic [Marx actually wrote "phantasmagorical"] form of a relation between things.' This is why Marx called commodities 'social hieroglyphs'. They require specialized interpretation (a 'critique of political economy') for their social meaning to become apparent. Commodities are hieroglyphs *because* of their peculiar fetish character.

If the tension between Marx's metaphors is anything to go by – with Egyptology following on fast here from the fetish, which in its sixteenth-century origins was a West Africa phenomenon – a commodity is indeed a very contradictory, mixed-up thing. Things are further complicated when Marx claims that in its relations with other commodities, a commodity 'stands on its head'. Inversion – turning something upside down, turning it on its head – was Marx's favourite metaphor for philosophical idealism and the religious world alike, since, for him, idealism was but a secular version of religious representation. Philosophical idealism treats concepts in the same way as religious thought treats supernatural entities: both prioritize ideal entities over material ones. Fetishism appears within this context as a category from the

Enlightenment philosophy of religion. The Enlightenment was an eighteenth-century cultural movement promoting secularization and the power of reason and empirical knowledge against clericalism, superstition and tradition. Within the terms of the Enlightenment philosophy of religion, fetishism is that type of 'primitive' social practice within which individual material things are attributed, or endowed with, supernatural powers and thereby acquire a special social value. It is a historically and anthropologically particular form of religious inversion.

From the perspective of the Enlightenment, fetishism is a distinctly pre-modern, and therefore irrational, phenomenon. Fetishism is one of a series of terms that Marx uses to characterize states of affairs that produce illusions, all of which derive from an Enlightenment discourse that relegates such illusions to the past. Others words used in this same section of *Capital* to refer to the effects of commodities, for example, include 'magic', 'necromancy', the 'mystical veil' and 'superstition'. Throughout Marx's writings, such terms are frequently combined with distinctively modern metaphors of optical illusion. In his early writings, for example, Marx used the image of the camera obscura, to describe ideology as a turning of the world upside-down. In the extract above, he evokes the phantasmagoria, a theatrical exhibition of optical illusions, mainly created by the magic lantern, which was first staged in London in 1802. There is a trick of the eye built into the very structure of the commodity-form, Marx is suggesting. It is an 'objective illusion' that remains even after it has been comprehended.

This combination of modern and pre-modern imagery is a distinctive feature of Marx's writing about capitalism. Marx draws upon a gothic literary imaginary, in presenting capitalism as secretly possessed by a series of pre-modern forms. But unlike in the gothic, these forms are not *residues* or *remnants* of earlier, feudal social forms, persisting, lurking repressed beneath the surface of modernity. They are effects of the most advanced economic form itself: capitalism. This is the germ of the idea that Max Horkheimer and Theodor W. Adorno would later, in the 1940s, formulate as the 'dialectic of enlightenment': pushed to its limit, enlightenment (here, commodity production as a rational harnessing of natural materials) is itself revealed to be bound up with myth (the fetishism of commodities).[2]

Marx first appealed to fetishism as a critical term in 1842, in the final paragraph of his article in the *Rhenish Times* on 'Debates on the Law on Thefts of Wood', having just read Charles de Brosses, *On the Cult of Fetish Gods, or the Parallel of Ancient Egyptian Religion with the Modern Religion of Negritie* (1760), in which Egypt and West Africa are explicitly compared. He would already have been familiar with Brosses's concept of fetishism from Hegel's *Lectures on the Philosophy of World History*, published posthumously in 1837, while Marx was a student moving in Hegelian circles in Berlin. (Eduard Gans, who prepared the edition, was someone whose classes Marx attended.) Hegel (1770–1831) discusses the fetish in his lecture on Africa, using the alleged slavish subordination of Africans to – crucially, arbitrarily chosen – fetishes as justification for the view that Africa 'is no part of the historical world', since it has 'no movement or development to exhibit'.[3]

De Brosses coined the word 'fetishism' (*fétichisme*) in 1757. He was the first to elaborate the concept as a general type of 'primitive mentality' and 'natural' religious practice. The term fetish (*fétiche*), from which he derived it, developed out of the pidgin term *fetisso* used in the coastal region of West Africa during the sixteenth and seventeenth centuries. It, in turn, derived from the late medieval Portugese word *feitico*, meaning magical practice or witchcraft. As such, fetishism is a quintessentially transcultural concept, the product of an encounter between radically different social and cultural systems: African lineage, Christian feudal and merchant capitalist. The term has its origins in trading, in exchange.[4]

In his article on the Rhine law on thefts of wood, Marx used the term 'fetish' in a straightforward Enlightenment manner, similar to Hegel, to criticize the 'abject materialism' of the Rhineland Province Assembly. He wrote:

> The *savages of Cuba* regarded gold as a *fetish of the Spaniards*. They celebrated a feast in its honour, sang in a circle around it and then threw it into the sea. If the Cuban savages had been present at the sitting of the Rhine Province Assembly, would they not have regarded *wood* as the *Rhinelanders' fetish*? (*MECW* 1, 262–3)

The Rhine forest owners, who dominated the assembly, Marx argued, were fixated on wood as the emblem of their private economic interest, irrespective of the general interest. As a result, when it came to debating the law on the theft of wood, they paid no heed to the general interest, which, as a political body, Marx believed the Assembly should have represented. This fixation of the owners of the forests on their private interests – wood – Marx wrote, 'abolishes all natural and spiritual distinctions by enthroning in their stead the immoral, irrational and soulless abstraction of a particular material object and a particular consciousness which is slavishly subordinated to this object'.

Marx's application of the concept of the fetish to the commodity-form in *Capital* is a significant theoretical development from this, since he applies it to commodities in general, irrespective of their material qualities. (Although, interestingly, his example of a commodity in the fetishism section of

Capital is a wooden table, providing a subterranean connection back to the article in the *Rhenish Times*.) He discards what was previously one of the main features of fetishism – its arbitrary materialism – thereby reducing it to animism more generally, which is the attribution of a living soul or spiritual substance to inanimate objects. Within Marx's account of capitalism, the fetishized commodity-form exhibits considerable 'movement and development' (unlike African societies in Hegel's account of them). Furthermore, this movement, which is internal to the value-form – from the commodity to money to capital – takes the conceptual form of Hegelian dialectic. (Hegel's dialectical logic formalized the understanding of change, by conceiving it as a process of the production and resolution of contradictions. Marx presented the value-form as developing in a similar way, from its equivalent and relative forms, via a general form, to the universal form of money.) The analogy of the fetish in *Capital* is thus much less strict than in Marx's earlier more conventional usage.

On the other hand, in locating fetishism at work in exchange, Marx can be seen to be (unknowingly) returning the concept to the social context of its historical formation: the encounter of Portugese traders with West African tribes in the sixteenth century. The concept of the fetish was the outcome of this encounter. It was used by the Portugese to explain an otherwise inexplicable attribution of value to certain African tribal objects. In this respect, Marx's use of it in *Capital* conforms to its founding transcultural function quite precisely. Commodity fetishism is not an instance of a lowly, because arbitrary, materialism (the standard Enlightenment view of the fetish), but of a peculiar and novel type of materially grounded social *idealism*. It is an effect of something 'purely social' – exchange-value – that nonetheless conceals its own social basis, in abstract labour. Hence its hieroglyphic character. It needs decoding. In contrast, the motives underlying the Rhine forest owners' fetishism of wood (defence of their private property) was plain for all to see. This difference marks the distinctively modern, capitalistic character of the social fetishism associated with commodities.

Where do these historical issues leave the critical force of Marx's concept of fetishism? Certainly, Marx's analysis raises as many problems as it solves. In using fetishism as a critical term, Marx is applying to the commodity-form the Enlightenment ideal of a world rendered transparent by scientific knowledge. Similarly, the metaphor of the hieroglyph, with its enigmatic or riddle-like character, identifies the commodity-form as something to be subjected to interpretation, a puzzle to be solved. Capitalist societies, Marx is saying, fail to live up to the Enlightenment ideal of rationality they claim to represent, because they are *opaque* to their members. The social relations of cooperation that structure the total labour of society are hidden behind the 'veil' of the merely quantitative relations between products. In this respect, the concept of commodity fetishism performs an internal critique of capitalism's aspirations to be a rational social form. Enlightenment, Marx was saying, cannot come about within capitalism, because capitalism produces social illusion as a result of its 'elementary' social form, the commodity. However, this reduces the criterion for historical judgements about societies to the transparency of their socio-economic structures. This is clear later on in this same section of *Capital*:

> The religious reflections of the actual world can vanish only when the practical relations of everyday life between people, and between humanity and nature, present themselves in a transparent and rational form. The social life-process, which is based on the material process of production, does not

strip off its mystical veil until it becomes production by
freely associated men and women, and stands under their
conscious and planned control. (*C* 1, 173)

Conscious and planned production by freely associated men
and women, in other words, communism, is recommended as
a condition for the transparency of the practical relations of
everyday life. Elsewhere in Marx's writings, communism has
more to do with freedom: the development and enjoyment by
individuals of the potentialities of the species (see chapter 6).
But the relationship between freedom and social transparency
remained unexplored.

   The transparency of social relations is only one of several
criteria that Marx used to make political and historical judgements about different societies. Nonetheless, its limits are
worth keeping in mind when thinking about the power of
commodity fetishism as a critical, rather than an analytical or
interpretative category in Marx's investigation of capitalism.
When he wrote of commodity fetishism Marx wrote not of a
desire for commodities but of a displacement of the desire
to know.

2

A NEW MATERIALISM (1): PRACTICE

1.

The chief defect of all hitherto existing materialism (that of Feuerbach included) is that objectivity, actuality, sensibility is conceived only in the form of the *object or of intuition*; but not as *sensible human activity, practice*, not subjectively. Hence, in opposition to materialism, the active side was developed abstractly by idealism – which naturally does not know actual, sensible activity as such. Feuerbach wants sensible objects – really distinguished from thought-objects: but he does not conceive human activity itself as *objective* activity . . . Hence he does not grasp the significance of 'revolutionary', practical-critical activity. . . .

6.

Feuerbach resolves the religious essence into the *human* essence. But the human essence is no abstraction inherent in each single individual. In its actuality it is the ensemble of social relations. Feuerbach, who does not enter into a critique of this actual essence, is hence compelled:

1. To abstract from the historical process and to fix the religious sentiment as something for itself and to presuppose an abstract-*isolated*-human individual.

2. Essence can therefore be conceived only as 'genus', inner, mute generality *naturally* uniting the many individuals. . . .

8.

All social life is essentially *practical*. All mysteries that lead theory to mysticism find their rational solution in human practice and in the comprehension of this practice.

9.

The highest point reached by intuitive materialism, that is the materialism that does not grasp sensibility as practical activity, is the observation of single individuals and of civil society.

10.

The standpoint of the old materialism is civil society, the standpoint of the new is human society or social humanity.

11.

Philosophers have only *interpreted* the world in various ways, the point is to *change* it.

Extract from 'On Feuerbach', 1845

'Philosophers have only *interpreted* the world in various ways, the point is to *change* it.' Marx's 'On Feuerbach' is justly famous for its concluding, exasperated cry to change the world. Marx was exasperated with philosophers. Usually, Marx criticized philosophers for their idealism. But here he was exasperated with what was at the time the very latest conception of materialism, Feuerbach's. He was exasperated that materialism – an idea Marx associated with human needs and interests and hence with conflict and action – should be only 'interpretative'. Marx used the German verb *interpretieren* here, which is common in the context of musical performance, where performers interpret a score, rather than the more philosophical term *verstehen*, with its stronger association with understanding.

Feuerbach had given materialism – traditionally the philosophical doctrine that nothing exists except matter – a humanistic inflection, by emphasizing the place of humanity within nature, and the 'givenness' of the world to the human senses. Marx's 'On Feuerbach' was the beginning of a new concept of materialism that goes beyond the idea of the world as a set of sensibly perceptible objects, to focus on our practical interactions with nature. Marx's new materialism aimed to do more than 'interpret' the world as it is given to us. It aimed to be intellectually adequate to the practical task of changing the world. It is the philosophical basis of Marx's mature thought.

Marx jotted down his notes 'On Feuerbach' in the spring of 1845, in Brussels, having recently been expelled from France as a political agitator, at the request of the Prussian authorities. It was first published over forty years later, after Marx's death, by his friend and collaborator Friedrich Engels, as an appendix to his own *Ludwig Feuerbach and the Exit from Classical German Philosophy* (1888). Marx's text is popularly known as the 'Theses on Feuerbach', after a remark of Engels's. But it is not really, strictly speaking, a set of theses, nor is it primarily about Feuerbach. Its form is important though – despite the haphazard status of the text – not least because it gives us a clue to its hidden philosophical ancestry in the messianic materialism of early German Romanticism. I shall thus briefly provide a literary context for the text before turning to the content of the extract.

In its literary form, 'On Feuerbach' is a collection of fragments, in the sense given to the term fragment by the early German Romantics: a short piece which, 'like a small work of art', is formally 'complete in itself', but nonetheless incomplete in its meaning. This incompleteness of meaning gives it the status of a project rather than an already realized truth.[5] The literary antecedent of 'On Feuerbach' is thus not so much Martin Luther's famous theses – nailed to the door of the church in Wittenberg in 1517 – as Friedrich Schlegel's collections of fragments published in the journal *The Athenaeum* between 1798 and 1800. In this respect, Marx's text is closer to those of Kierkegaard and Nietzsche (the pre-eminent late nineteenth-century successor to philosophical Romanticism, whose aphorisms extend the fragment form), or even Baudelaire, than to the medieval disputations out of which the theses form evolved. This is especially true of the special type of individuality associated with fragments, whereby thoughts with a universal scope ('All social life . . . All mysteries . . .') are reduced to crystalline, gnomic propositions ('. . . is essentially practical . . . find their rational solution in . . .'). Such sentences move productively, but enigmatically, between the closed wholeness of an image, produced by their brevity – they can be apprehended in a glance – and the open infinity of their meaning. This movement between two types of apprehension (completeness of form and incompleteness of meaning) is understood to produce an impulse towards action because the actualization of the ideas at stake is taken to require something more than conceptual representation. They must find some other outlet, in the intuitive and existential dimensions of experience, in art, in 'life' and in politics. This is the messianic aspect of early Romanticism: the prospect – and it is only a prospect, a hope, a horizon, not an empirically justifiable belief – of a practice that might actualize philosophical ideas.

The fragment (like the notebook within which it is enclosed) is a distinctively modern literary form. For the early Romantics, it was *the* modern form, of which the novel is but an extended variant. It is at once a document of reflective introspection and a glimpse of the world as a whole. It attains truth by virtue of the accompaniment of its subjective will to truth with an objective, formal self-awareness of its own partiality – its fragmentary status. The posthumously published philosophical notebook – unfinished and thereby necessarily fragmentary in form – stands at the forefront of philosophical modernity. Marx's 'On Feuerbach' is in this respect a slender contribution to a German tradition that includes Nietzsche's *Will to Power* (1883–8), Heidegger's *Contributions to Philosophy* (1936–8), Benjamin's *Arcades Project* (1927–40) and Wittgenstein's *Philosophical Investigations* (1929–49), all of which have a special status despite (or rather precisely because of) their status as unfinished works, unpublished in the lifetimes of their authors. If the theoretical content of these texts is dense, at times to the point of enigma, the form of their incompleteness is nonetheless crucial for projecting a unity to the bodies of work to which they are appended. A slender sheet, 'On Feuerbach' allows us, retrospectively, to unify Marx's writings philosophically as a social materialism of practice – a transformation of Feuerbach's concept of materialism by the concepts of practice and the social. This is the idea we need to understand.

Feuerbach functions in Marx's notes as a foil for the thrust of his own thought, a name for a polemically simplified position, an archetypical straw-man. It is Feuerbach's unhappy fate to have entered posterity primarily as the butt of Marx's criticisms, as a figure of the transition in Marx's development away from traditional philosophy towards the study of history, economics and politics, and only secondarily as a critic of religion and a philosophical figure in his own right. For Marx, Feuerbach is the most sophisticated contemporary representative of the 'old' materialism.[6]

The first thing to note about Marx's text is that it appears to have little to do with the traditional philosophical doctrine of materialism: the idea that there is only one 'substance' in the world, matter, and everything else (thought, for example) is a modification or an attribute of it. Neither what Marx called the old materialism 'of the object or of intuition' nor his own new materialism of practice are metaphysics of matter in this old-fashioned sense. This is important because after Marx's death, Engels and subsequently Soviet Marxists claimed that Marx propounded a new version of traditional philosophical materialism that they called 'dialectical materialism' and which became known as 'diamat', for short. It is a combination of a traditional metaphysical materialism of matter with Hegel's dialectical logic (which is a logic of process or change). Dialectical materialism holds that the world is fundamentally made up of 'matter in motion'. Generations of Soviet-style Marxists were educated in the fixed, doctrinal formulas of dialectical materialism and its twin, historical materialism, or 'histomat', which was taken to be its 'scientific' companion, the science of history.[7] Marx's new materialism is certainly concerned with movement, but it is a subjective movement, what he calls 'sensible human activity, practice', not the inhuman movement of matter according to laws of nature. It is a materialism of what philosophers call 'the subject' – the I, the one who knows and acts, the principle of activity. In 'On Feuerbach', Marx offered a new philosophical definition of the subject.

He did this by drawing upon, reorganizing and giving new uses to a set of terms and concepts that have their origin in the philosophy of Immanuel Kant (1724–1804), and are also at work in Feuerbach's writings. In the first of Marx's fragments, the German terms for 'objectivity', 'sensibility' and 'intuition' are all everyday words that were given technical meanings in Kant's writings and then passed into the tradition of German philosophy. In particular, Marx is drawing upon and transforming

Kant's famous 'subjective' redefinition of objectivity. Kant argued that the object of knowledge should no longer be conceived as something completely independent of the knowing subject (the I, the one who knows). Ultimately, for Kant, this is an incoherent idea, because if the object of knowledge was completely independent of the subject, how could it ever be known by it? Instead, Kant suggested, what makes knowledge possible is the existence of certain common mental structures, *within* the subject. Such knowledge, whilst subjective in form, nonetheless has objective validity in so far as these structures can be shown to be universal and necessary elements of all possible knowledge. Among the things that Kant claimed are structures of this kind are space, time and causality. For Kant, these are human contributions to the intelligibility of the world; they are within *us* (subjects), as ways of making sense of what exists. They don't exist independently of us.

Marx's attack on all previous materialism is in line with Kant's identification of knowledge as the product of the cognitive activity of the subject. Marx acknowledged this connection when he wrote that 'in opposition to materialism, the active side was developed abstractly by idealism'. However, unlike Kant, Marx does not conceive of the activity of the subject (the I, the one who knows and acts) as separate from its sensibility or sensuousness. In this respect, Kant viewed human understanding and thinking in a dual manner. For Kant, sensibility was always passive and intuitive. Rather, Marx conceives activity as *itself* sensible – something that idealism, which restricts activity to thought, 'naturally does not know'. Marx's practical extension of Kant's subjective turn (placing the activity of the subject at the centre of the production of knowledge) involves a rejection of a notion shared by Kant and Feuerbach alike: the passivity of the sensible. This is what Marx refers to as the 'old' materialist conception of 'sensibility conceived only in the form of the object or of intuition'.

In this respect, the first fragment of 'On Feuerbach' cuts through prevailing understandings of the conceptual pair, 'subject' and 'object', on which theories of knowledge had been based since Descartes (1596–1650). It dissociates the subject from representation, from its restriction to being a subject only of knowledge, and redefines it as 'sensible' activity or social practice. In the summary formulation of the French philosopher Étienne Balibar: 'the subject is practice . . . *the subject is nothing other than practice* which has always already begun and continues indefinitely'.[8] We are now in a position to understand the significance of 'practical-critical' or 'revolutionary' activity, which Marx claimed that Feuerbach 'does not grasp': it is an expression of the practical, transformative character of human sub-jectivity itself. To put it another way, for Marx, to engage in 'practical-critical' or 'revolutionary' activity is not an occasional or aberrant occupation, it is part of what it means to be human.

This new materialist redefinition of the human subject as sensible practice (practical activity as the sensuous being of the human), rather than a subject defined by its knowledge of an object, has profound consequences for the traditional philosophical concept of the human essence. For rather than being an 'abstraction inherent in each single individual' (what all humans have in common), 'an inner, mute generality *naturally* uniting the many individuals', the essence or unity of the human must now be considered to be distributed *relationally* among all humans. This is what Marx meant when he wrote that 'in its actuality it is the ensemble of social relations'. As Balibar has pointed out, Marx used the French term 'ensemble' here, in all likelihood in order to distance himself from the implications of a hierarchical completeness associated, philosophically, with the German terms for totality (*Totalität*) and whole (*Ganze*). An ensemble is more of a fluid network of relations.

Humanity can no longer be viewed as a collection of disparate individuals united by a common natural essence, which is inherent mutely within each of them. This was the standpoint of the old materialism, equivalent to that of civil society, for which the social is but the sum of interactions between competing individuals. The new materialism adopts the relational standpoint of 'human society or social humanity'. It is the relational and hence, ironically, 'ideal' character of sociality that moves Marx's idea beyond all previous, old materialisms: both the traditional metaphysical materialism of 'matter' and Feuerbach's more Kantian materialism of the 'object of intuition'. For Marx, society is not a thing; it is a structured network of relations in flux.

The question of how a network of relations in flux can be encompassed within a view that calls itself 'materialism' is frustratingly left unaddressed by Marx in these fragments. He simply stresses the sensible character of human practices. But these are social only because they relate to each other, rather than because of their sensuous materiality. Marx's concept of practice ('sensible human activity') remains abstract. We are not told how social relations themselves might be explained 'materially'. That account is deferred. What the fragments 'On Feuerbach' do leave us with, however, is a clear series of conceptual oppositions between the old and the new materialism. This polemical series of oppositional pairs is best expressed diagrammatically. It articulates two separate lines of thought.

Old materialism	New materialism
Passive, sensible intuition	Sensible-human activity/ objective activity = practice
The object	The subject
Abstract	Concrete
Isolated individual	Social relations
Natural	Social
Civil society	Human society/social humanity
Matter	Materiality of the social?

This series of oppositions underlies, and gives meaning to, the concluding, eleventh fragment: 'Philosophers have only *interpreted* the world in various ways, the point is to *change* it.'

The eleventh fragment takes up the elusive reference to 'the significance of "revolutionary", practical–critical activity' with which the first fragment ends. If the activity that makes the subject human is both 'sensible' and 'objective', it will transform the world of objects. To exist as human is thus not merely to know, inhabit and subsist within the world (the standpoint of the old materialism), but to change it. '"Revolutionary", practical–critical activity' is directed *specifically* towards changing the world. It is a reflexively transformative practice. We should avoid attributing to Marx an exclusive opposition between understanding and changing the world. Philosophers, however, have *only* interpreted the world. And in interpreting the world only from the standpoint of 'the object or of intuition', rather than practice, they have misinterpreted it. Changing the world, on the other hand, is both the point (*telos*, end) of human activity and the appropriate perspective from which to understand it.

The perspective of change reveals the human as an on-going process that takes ever-changing forms. Its unity is not given but must be produced. Furthermore, to view human activity from the standpoint of change (rather than preservation or simple reproduction) is to view human activity historically. Marx made this connection explicitly a few months later, in November 1845, when, in the first part of *The German Ideology*, he returned to Feuerbach to write (as if in summary of the argument of his fragments): 'As far as Feuerbach is a materialist he does not deal with history, and as far as he considers history he is not a materialist. With him materialism and history diverge completely.' (*MECW* 5, 41) By rendering explicit the historical character of the new materialism, Marx set the stage for a derivation of a new concept of history, and thereby, in the process, the completion of his new concept of materialism itself.

3

A NEW MATERIALISM (2): HISTORY

The first premise of all human history is naturally the existence of living human individuals. Thus the first fact to be established is the physical organization of these individuals and their consequent relation to the rest of nature . . . All historical writing must set out from these natural bases and their modification in the course of history through the action of men and women.

Humans can be distinguished from animals by consciousness, by religion or anything else you like. They themselves begin to distinguish themselves from animals as soon as they begin to *produce* their means of subsistence, a step that is conditioned by their physical organization. By producing their means of subsistence humans are indirectly producing their material life.

The way in which men and women produce their means of subsistence depends first of all on the nature of the means of subsistence they actually find in existence and have to reproduce.

This mode of production must not be considered simply as being the reproduction of the physical existence of the individuals. Rather it is a definite form of activity of these individuals, a definite form of expressing their life, a definite *way of life* on their part. As individuals express their life, so they are. What they are, therefore, coincides with their production, both with *what* they produce and with *how* they produce. Hence what individuals are depends on the material conditions of their production . . .

The first historical act is thus the production of the means to satisfy these [existing] needs, the production of material life itself. And indeed this is an historical act, a fundamental condition of all history, which today, as thousands of years ago, must daily and hourly be fulfilled merely in order to sustain human life . . .

The second point is that the satisfaction of the first need, the action of satisfying and the instrument of satisfaction that has been acquired, leads to new needs; and this creation of new needs is the first historical act . . .

The third relation which, from the very outset, enters into historical development, is that men and women, who daily re-create their own life, begin to make other men and women, to propagate their kind: the relation between man and woman, parents and children, the *family* . . .

These three sides of social activity are not of course to be taken as three different stages, but just as three sides, or to make it clear to the Germans, three 'moments', which have existed simultaneously since the dawn of history and the first humans, and which still assert themselves in history today.

Extract from 'Opposition of the Materialist and Idealist Outlook',
Marx/Engels, *The German Ideology*, 1845/6

Marx's first philosophical innovation was a transformation of the old materialist conception of the world as a realm of objects perceived by the senses to include a 'subjective' aspect, which he described as 'sensible human activity' or 'practice'. However, in 'On Feuerbach', Marx gave no indication of how the sensible or material dimension of human activity is to be understood. There is reference to 'social relations' (as opposed to a 'natural essence') uniting human individuals, but the sense in which these relations are themselves 'material', and their role in structuring human activity are not dealt with. Marx's first formulation of his new practical materialism was incomplete. It is as if he had simply added the concepts of 'the subject' (activity) and 'the social' (relations) to the old object-based model, almost arithmetically, without laying the groundwork for their conjunction or working through its implications. The sense in which Marx's new materialism involves an expansion in the *concept* of materialism (as opposed to being an idealistically enhanced version of Feuerbach's materialism) was still unclear in the spring of 1845. Clarification was the task of the first part of *The German Ideology*, written in collaboration with Engels, and begun a few months after they returned from a trip to England in the summer of 1845, to study English economic writings unavailable in Brussels.

The German Ideology is the first of Marx and Engels's co-authored works that was genuinely collaborative. They had begun working together a year earlier, when Engels visited Marx in Paris for ten days at the end of August 1844. However, the joint work that was the eventual product of that visit, *The Holy Family or Critique of Critical Criticism: Against Bruno Bauer and Company* (1845), was a combination of individually composed parts. Engels wrote his part during his brief ten-day stay. *The German Ideology*, on the other hand, was the result of an intensive process of joint composition, with Marx performing the final editorial function.

The German Ideology is famous, first, for being the founding text of 'historical materialism', and second, for having been 'willingly abandoned to the gnawing criticism of the mice'. Its prospective publishers, the Westphalian entrepreneurs Julius Meyer and Rudolph Rempel, withdrew their funds when the manuscript was already at the printers in the summer of 1846. Perhaps this was because they discovered that their own political position (ironically designated by Marx and Engels as 'true socialism') was castigated in the text. Perhaps also because at over five hundred pages (two-thirds of which are dedicated to the critique of a single book by a contemporary, Max Stirner) publication no longer looked an attractive venture. Either way, by July 1846 Meyer and Rempel claimed that their money was tied up elsewhere.[9] Engels rediscovered the manuscript among Marx's possessions after his death and drew upon it extensively in his own later writings. 'We were bold devils then,' he wrote to Marx's youngest daughter Laura, in June 1883, on rereading one of the more polemical chapters, 'Heine's poetry is childlike innocence compared with our prose' (*MECW* 47, 30). The full text was not published until 1932, in Moscow. By the mid-1960s, *The German Ideology* had become a set text for the *agrégation* in philosophy in France (a national competitive examination for teachers). More recently, the opening section, 'Opposition of the Materialist and Idealist Outlook', from which this extract is taken, became part of the syllabus for an A level examination in philosophy in England.

The reason Marx gave, retrospectively, for his willingness to abandon the attempt to get the manuscript published was that it had already achieved its main purpose: 'self-clarification'. In *The German Ideology*, the concept of material interests – the importance of which Marx had first recognized while covering debates in the Rhine Province Assembly for the *Rhenish Times* and which had led him to study political economy – is brought together with the notion of practice from 'On Feuerbach' to complete Marx's new conception of materialism.

The second stage in the development of Marx's concept of materialism is broadly speaking, 'economic'. Marxism is associated in the popular imagination with economics, and there is a corresponding, largely derogatory, everyday sense of the term materialism, associated with the immediate satisfaction of material needs and desires. This is the sense in which capitalist societies are described as 'materialistic', for example, by virtue of the dominance within everyday life of the economic imperatives to produce and to consume, and a corresponding decline in the social authority of other, more spiritual, ethical norms. However, the account of the 'materialist outlook' in *The German Ideology* does not take the form of an economic treatise, in any conventional sense.

The 'economics' generally taught in schools and universities today concerns itself with only a very narrowly defined range of economic activity ('market behaviour') characteristic of one particular kind of society, capitalist society. In Marx's work, on the other hand, the economic aspect of human life is considered to be the foundation of humanity's *social being*. Marx treated the economic as the link between the biological and social aspects of the human. In looking to the biological basis of social relations, Marx reconnected human practice to a traditional philosophical materialism of 'matter', since organic life may be considered the product of a particular organization of matter. By viewing natural instincts and needs as only the basis – but not in themselves the content – of social relations, however, he retained the primacy of practice, which he had asserted in 'On Feuerbach'. It is in the relationship between the 'natural' and the 'social' aspects of the economic that the core of Marx's materialism lies. It is the dynamism of this relationship that is understood to give rise to history. Hence the conventional designation of Marx's materialism as a 'materialist conception of history'. Indeed, in the first version of the clean copy of the manuscript of *The German Ideology*, the first section begins: 'We know only a single science, the science of history.' Marx's new concept of materialism led him to history, not to economics, in any disciplinary sense. And as the passage that immediately follows this sentence shows, this was an expanded – indeed, all-embracing – conception of history:

> One can look at history from two sides and divide it into the history of nature and the history of humanity. The two sides are, however, inseparable; the history of nature and the history of humans are dependent on each other so long as humankind exists.[10]

Our extract begins with a new, *natural-historical* definition of the human. Rather than seeking a particular attribute (or set of attributes) that distinguishes humans from other animals – as one might if one were to treat animal species as objects, along the lines of the 'old' materialism – Marx reformulated the question. It became a question about the basis on which humans historically distinguish themselves from other animals. Marx's answer was that humans distinguish themselves from other animal species 'as soon as they begin to *produce* their means of subsistence'. Marx viewed the economic as an ontological category of the human ('ontology' is the systematic study of being or what is): the social production of means of subsistence is the production of the human itself. The assumption is that other animals have an immediate, instinctual metabolic interaction with nature, but that there came a point in the development of the biological species that subsequently became 'human' when existing needs began to be satisfied in a new way, by the transformation of nature via social co-operation. All other distinguishing attributes of the human (such as consciousness, religion, language, reason, etc), Marx suggested, have their source in this one, more fundamental, practical natural-historical feature.

This definition is 'natural-historical' because it concerns an act – production – that is *simultaneously* natural and historical. It is natural in so far as it is premised upon the 'physical organization' of 'living human individuals' and their prior immediate subsistence on nature: need and its satisfaction. It is historical in so far as the social production of means to satisfy this same need may be considered 'the first historical act'. Marx identified need as the material basis of the social relations that unite 'the many human individuals'. This is what was missing from the account of practical materialism in 'On Feuerbach'. But it is not the only 'material' content of those social relations. It is not only a question of *what* is produced, but of *how* it is produced: the means and the modes of social co-operation. Social co-operation has a material content too: both the means or instruments of production available at any particular time in history and the forms of social authority organizing production impose limitations on the movements of human bodies in space and time within the production process. They give 'material content' to the social relations of production, and they can come into conflict with them. It is this conflict, in Marx's view, that gives history its movement.

In little more than a page of *The German Ideology*, the new practical concept of materialism that Marx introduced in 'On Feuerbach' has undergone a complex development. Its main concept, 'sensible human activity, practice', has been, first, reduced to its most basic form, 'the production of the means of subsistence'; and next, analytically broken down into its 'natural', 'social' and 'historical' aspects, respectively, in a complicated structure of relations that now define 'the human'. It is the concept of the historical that is the most difficult. If 'history' is to have a more specific meaning than the simple passage of time, such that it makes sense to think of the emergence of history out of nature, there must be a temporal logic to practice that transcends its natural conditions. There must be a time of social action that is different from the time of nature: a time of past, present and future, as well as a simple succession of instants. The temporality of action is a narrative temporality of events, bounded and given meaning by the prospective death of the human subjects involved. The temporality of nature, on the other hand, is indifferent to human life and death alike.[11]

One reason for the difficulty here in understanding Marx's conception of the historical aspect of the human is that he appears to contradict himself by offering two quite different descriptions of 'the first historical act'. It is tempting, at this point, to evoke the unpublished and hence still provisional character of the manuscript. (It may have reached the printers, but Marx and Engels had not had proofs.) But this would leave the problem unresolved and, in any case, it is unnecessary. It makes more sense to read the two descriptions together, in their contradictory unity, as descriptions of different aspects of a single act. When Marx writes that the first historical act is 'the production of the means to satisfy these [existing] needs', he can be glossed as saying this is the first human, social act: the act by virtue of which humans emerge out of the rest of nature as a new kind of being. But he has not yet specified precisely what is distinctively 'historical' about this being. At this point in the argument, it is the social aspect of the human that is the differentiating factor. The social character of production distinguishes the human relation to nature from that of other animals.

It is only with 'the second point' that a distinctively historical temporality is introduced. Marx claims that satisfying the 'first [existing] need' with a new 'instrument of satisfaction' (some social means) leads to '*new* needs': first of all, a need for this new instrument (a tool, for example). It is this 'creation of new needs' that is the first historical act. The first historical act leads to a renewal of the production of means of production – Marx will later call this social reproduction. One of the main forms of production in any society is the production of means of production – nowadays, the production of the machines needed to make other products. Marx's grammar is confusing (the manuscript never received its final revision), but there is only one act at issue here. The 'production of the means to satisfy existing needs' and the 'creation of new needs' refer to two aspects of the same act, since the production of new means to satisfy existing needs creates a (hitherto non-existent) need for these means. The creation of new needs introduces a specifically *historical* logic into what was previously only a *social* conception of the human because it introduces a new type of social measure: the development of human needs and the forces of production that correspond to them. To be human, for Marx, is to create new needs. History is the process of expansion of human needs and the productive forces corresponding to them.

'On Feuerbach' staged a move from a naturalistic conception of the human to a practical and social one. *The German Ideology* develops this practical and social conception of the human into an economic and a historical one. The economic is the ontological content of the historical: the production of new needs. As Marx put it a little further on, polemicizing against what he calls the 'German' tendency to prioritize politics and religion within history:

> . . . there exists a materialist connection between human beings caused by their needs and their mode of production . . . that is as old as men and women themselves. This

connection is ever taking on new forms and thus presents a 'history' irrespective of the existence of any political or religious nonsense which would especially hold human beings together.

The third and final social aspect of this 'materialist connection' identified by Marx concerns the relations governing the biological reproduction of the species, the relations of procreation, or the family. Historically, this aspect comes first, since it develops initially on a natural basis within the 'pre-historical' life of the species. To begin with, Marx wrote, the family is 'the only social relation'. However, 'when increased needs create new social relations and the increased population new needs', the family becomes a 'subordinate' relation. '[It] must then be treated and analysed according to the existing empirical data, not according to "the concept of the family", as is the custom in German.' Despite its 'natural' beginnings, the family is thus a historical form, which changes in line with changes in economic relations – as is evident from the statistics about changing patterns of child-rearing and living arrangements in capitalist societies today.

So, Marx's natural-historical definition of the human is at the same time a socio-historical one. Within human life, biological needs acquire new, social objects of satisfaction. As Marx put it in the paragraph that follows on from the extract:

The production of life, both of one's own in labour and of fresh life in procreation, now appears as a two-fold relation: on the one hand as a natural, and on the other as a social relation – social in the sense that it denotes the co-operation of several individuals, no matter under what conditions, in what manner and to what end. It follows from this that a certain mode of production, or industrial stage, is always combined with a certain mode of co-operation, or social stage, and this mode of co-operation is itself a 'productive force'. Further, the aggregate of productive forces accessible to men and women conditions the social situation, hence, the 'history of humanity' must always be studied and treated in relation to the history of industry and exchange.

Marx's materialism does not lead to a historical determinism – the idea that historical events have sufficient causes and are thus in principle, though not in practice, predictable. It is not naturalism – it doesn't treat history as if it were governed by the same kinds of laws as nature – although it has naturalistic elements. Rather, material conditions (natural and social) are constraints that delimit a range of possibilities for human action. Marx's materialist conception of history provides a theoretical orientation that is intended to structure empirical research into historical process, and it is open to modification by the results of that research. But it is the fact that the social relations that structure 'sensible human activity' have a material content that makes sociological and historical explanation possible.[12]

On the other hand, the kinds of practice that Marx discussed in *The German Ideology* also have a more 'purely' social aspect, distinct *meanings*, irreducible to their natural and social functions, which derive from the way in which they are experienced by the subjects concerned. Marx referred to practices as 'expressions' of definite 'ways of life'. Here, he voiced a Romantic idea *within* his materialist conception of history. His conception of economics is a type of historical anthropology. It is the manner in which particular 'ways of life' express themselves, and in particular the misrepresentations of themselves that this involves, which is grasped by the concept of ideology. (Ideologies are systems of ideas that misrepresent society, which are intrinsically connected to certain social practices.) For Marx at this time, German philosophy was *the* German ideology because it was the primary means through which German culture (mis)represented the world to itself – by repressing its 'material conditions'. By the time he came to write *Capital*, however, in which it was no longer nations that were the relevant unit of analysis, but abstract economic forms themselves, Marx had come to the far harsher conclusion that the commodity form was its *own* ideology. It is part of the functioning of the commodity as a social form that it produces misrepresentations of itself. This is its fetish character. This kind of argument radically reduces the political significance of the type of polemic against 'ideologues' pursued by Marx and Engels in the main part of *The German Ideology*. In so far as there is a distinct set of ideas justifying the *status quo* that needs criticizing, it is not to be found in philosophy; rather, it is the discourse of political economy itself.

4

CRITIQUE OF POLITICAL ECONOMY: ALIENATION

Political economy proceeds from the fact of private property; it does not explain it. It expresses in general, abstract formulae the *material* process through which private property actually passes, which it then takes as *laws*. It does not *comprehend* these laws, i.e., it does not show how they arise from the nature of private property. Political economy fails to explain the reason for the division between labour and capital, and between capital and land . . .

[W]e have to grasp the essential connection between private property, greed, the separation of labour, capital and landed property, exchange and competition, value and the devaluation of men, monopoly and competition, etc. – the connection between this entire system of estrangement and the *money* system. . . .

We shall start out from a *present-day* economic fact. The worker becomes poorer the more wealth he produces, the more his production increases in power and extent. The worker becomes an ever-cheaper commodity the more commodities he produces . . .

This fact simply means that the object that labour produces, its product, stands opposed to it as *something alien*, as a *power independent* of the producer. The product of labour is labour embodied and made material in an object, it is the *objectification* of labour. The realization of labour is its objectification. Under these economic conditions, this realization of labour appears as loss of reality for the worker, objectification as *loss of and bondage to* the object, and appropriation as *estrangement*, as *alienation*. . . .

Political economy conceals the estrangement inherent in the nature of labour by ignoring the direct *relationship between the* worker *(labour) and production* . . . But estrangement manifests itself not only in the result, but also in the *act of production*, within the *activity of production* itself. How could the product of the worker's activity confront him as something alien if it were not for the fact that in the act of production he was estranging himself from himself? After all, the product is simply the summary of the activity, of the production. So if the product of labour is alienation, production itself must be active alienation, the alienation of activity, the activity of alienation. The estrangement of the object of labour merely summarizes the estrangement, the alienation in the activity of labour itself. . . .

We now have to derive a third feature of *estranged labour* from the two we have already looked at.

Humanity is a generic-being, not only because it practically and theoretically makes the genus – both its own and those of other things – its object, but also – and this is simply another way of saying the same thing – because it looks upon itself as the actual living genus, because it looks upon itself as a universal and therefore free being . . . The universality of humanity appears in practice in that universality which makes the whole of nature its *inorganic* body, (1) as a direct means of life, and (2) as the matter, the object, and the instrument of its life activity . . .

Estranged labour thus turns *humanity's generic-being* – both nature and humanity's spiritual generic-powers – into a being *alien* to it and a means of *individual existence*. It estranges humanity from its own body, from nature as it exists outside of it, from its spiritual essence, its *human* essence.

An immediate consequence of men and women's estrangement from the product of their labour, their life activity, their generic-being, is the *estrangement of men and women from other men and women* . . . each is estranged from the others and all are estranged from humanity's essential nature.

Extract from *Economic and Philosophical Manuscripts*, 1844

Political economy (or 'national economy', as it was known in Prussia at the time) was the economic science of Marx's day. What is generally referred to as economics today is a variant of the neo-classical economics that developed in Europe from the 1870s onwards. Neo-classical economics focuses on individual market behaviour within a narrowly defined set of assumptions about the independence of economic activity from political institutions – the so-called free market. Political economy, on the other hand, had a far wider scope. It included the philosophical definition of wealth, the theory of value, the accumulation and distribution of surpluses, the political arrangements necessary to promote accumulation, and an economic theory of historical progress.

Marx began to study political economy at the end of 1843 as a result of his criticism of Hegel's political philosophy and, in particular, its inadequacy to the development of an effective radical-democratic politics – Marx's preoccupation at the time. These criticisms led Marx to the famous conclusion set down retrospectively, in the 1859 Preface to his *Contribution to a Critique of Political Economy*: namely, that

neither legal relations nor political forms could be comprehended, whether by themselves or on the basis of a
so-called general development of the human mind (*Geist*),
but that on the contrary they originate in the material conditions of life, the totality of which Hegel, following the
example of English and French thinkers of the eighteenth
century, embraces within the term 'civil society'. The
anatomy of this civil society has to be sought in political
economy. (*MECW* 29, 262)[13]

Political economy became Marx's key to unlock the secret of
politics.

However, political economy was founded on the existing
economic forms ('the fact of private property') – the new
capitalistic forms of production for the market that emerged in
Europe in the course of the sixteenth and seventeenth centuries and developed, paradigmatically, during the industrial
revolution in England. Indeed, the primary purpose of political economy was to *justify* this economic system by
demonstrating its general social benefits. In so far as political
economy presupposed workers' lack of ownership of means of
production other than their own labour, it was in conflict
with Marx's egalitarian political goals. So, in turning to political economy for an analysis of civil society, Marx needed not
merely to study it, but to criticize it as well.

Marx's initial study of political economy was a two-fold
operation of appropriation and critique. He found his
inspiration for criticism in an article by Engels, 'Outlines of
a Critique of Political Economy', written in the autumn of
1843, and sent to Marx to be published in the journal he
was then setting up in Paris, the *German-French Yearbook*.
However, Engels's critique was more or less exclusively political – he described political economy as 'an entire science of

'enrichment' (*MECW* 3, 418) – and it was little more than a schema in form. Marx followed Engels in focusing on the place of the worker within the production process, but he added crucial philosophical depth to this approach by rethinking the concept of labour in its broadest human significance. By shifting the terms of political economy into this context, Marx was able to produce a critical account of the alienation produced by an economy based on wage-labour – a picture of the capitalist economy as an 'entire system of estrangement'.

Marx's account of alienation combines an intuitive appeal to the alienating character of waged work (who has not felt in some way alienated by their job?) with a complex philosophical analysis and a notoriously difficult vocabulary, derived from Hegel. More specifically, Marx articulated a four-fold existential sense of estrangement and loss, which he explained with reference to 'the fact of private property' in the means of production. This was no small task. Understanding it today is made more difficult by our historical distance from both its intellectual context and the terminology Marx used. Understanding it in English is especially difficult because there are *two* German words at stake, which were used in the eighteenth century as alternative translations of the single English word 'alienation', each of which grasps one distinct aspect of its meaning.[14] A brief digression on the history of the concept of alienation and its role in Hegel's philosophy is necessary to prepare us for reading this extract from Marx.

The basic meaning of the English term alienation is 'the action of making alien or other' (from the Latin, *alius*, other; and *alienus*, belonging to another person or place). Its main application in the early modern period was to the transfer of rights. In the natural law contract theory of Grotius (1583–1645), for example, it refers to the transfer of sovereign authority over oneself to another person, in exchange for the benefits of a stable social order – the transfer of sovereignty to a monarch. Later, in political economy, it refers to the transfer of property from one person to another, mainly (but not exclusively) in the form of buying and selling. It is the difference between these two contexts that generated the difference in meaning that is expressed in German in two different words. In the context of natural law theory, alienation had the negative connotation of loss, where an original freedom was given up or estranged. This is grasped by the German translation of alienation as *Entfremdung* (from *fremd*, alien). *Entfremdung* was first used to refer to theft and to the loss of mental powers, in the sense of a coma or a stupor, but gradually came to stand for a more general estrangement between persons. Nowadays, it is usually rendered into English as 'estrangement'. In the context of political economy, on the other hand (within which commodity exchange is considered an exchange of equivalents, hence, *without* loss), alienation had the more neutral sense of something becoming 'external' to its owner, through divestiture or sale. Hence the use of the German word *Entäusserung*, meaning 'externalization' (from *ausser*, outer or external).

Hegel took over and reunified this two-fold semantic legacy by incorporating it into his thought to describe a process whereby we come to know ourselves only through our externalization, or self-alienation, in objects. For externalization you can read 'objectification': the process by which a subject manifests itself in the form of an object, as the result of its activity. In Marx's words, 'the product is simply the summary of the activity, of the production', and, we might add, the production is always the manifestation of a subject – under the conditions of a division of labour, a *collective* subject, which Marx would later call the 'collective worker'. All human activity is objectification in this sense: objects are endowed with meanings as a result of the activities of which they are a part.

This externalization is an estrangement, for Hegel, in so far as consciousness (which for Hegel is ideal activity) knows itself only in the form of an object, as a mere result. However, for Hegel, this estrangement is only one stage in a longer process, through which consciousness eventually comes to recognize itself as a subject *within* the otherness of its objects. Hegel called this moment 'absolute self-recognition in absolute otherness' and it is the pinnacle of his thought. It need not concern us here, although we will return to this final moment of recovery when we discuss communism in chapter six.

Marx's innovation was to transfer the normative definition of alienation as estrangement and loss into the context of political economy, where it had previously had a more neutral sense, on the basis of Hegel's idea of objectification. In Hegelian terms, workers 'objectify' themselves in the products of their labour. Workers *are*, workers *exist* as workers, in labouring activity – be it agricultural work, factory work, office work, or by working in a shop or a call centre. The products of this work represent our main life-activity, however little we may personally care about these products or feel attached to them. Marx claimed that these objectifications stand 'opposed' to us as something alien, as an 'independent power', because we are socially separated from them by the fact of private property: under conditions of wage-labour (where workers are separated from the conditions of production by the fact that they are privately owned by someone else), workers have no rights of ownership over what they produce. These products possess a power because they embody the labour-power that produced them, in the form of value. In a capitalist economy, value is a measure of social power. This is why Marx wrote that the 'realization of labour appears as loss of reality for the worker'. The product has no reality for the workers who produce it because once produced it no longer has anything to do with them.

This is the first of Marx's four aspects or features of alienated labour – alienation of the product – all of which stem from the fact of wage-labour. Marx began his critique with the alienation of the product because it is the one most obviously connected to private property – the worker does not own the product. It is also the one that most directly corresponds to the structure of Hegel's account of objectification. But it is not the most significant, either existentially or theoretically. The second feature of alienated labour is the alienation of the activity, which is more basic than the alienation of the product: after all, 'the product is simply the summary of the activity'. In selling our labour-power for a discrete period of time, we give up the right to determine the goals or ends of our activity during that period. Within certain bounds, you cannot freely determine what you do while at work. Both the goals and the means of achieving them are externally imposed – by a manager, a supervisor or a foreman who represent the interests of the owner of the means of production. This is the most existentially immediate form of alienation: loss of control over the activity of labouring itself. It is the form of alienation most likely to produce resistance on the part of workers, the form most likely to lead to organization and struggle. Hence the integral role of trade unionism within the structure of the capitalist labour process: trade unions are the negotiators of the degrees of our 'unfreedom'.

The relationship between alienation and freedom is spelt out most explicitly in the third aspect of alienated labour discussed by Marx: the alienation of workers from their participation in humanity's 'generic-being'. Feuerbach's idea of humanity as a generic-being is the second philosophical source of Marx's theory of alienation. And just as Marx transformed Hegel's concept of objectification by placing it in the context of private property, so Marx also transformed Feuerbach's conception of humanity as a generic-being, by viewing it from the standpoint of labour.

Feuerbach conceived humans as essentially natural and sensuous (rather than ideal and spiritual) beings. Nonetheless, he maintained Hegel's rationalist belief that humanity has a special power, the universal power of thought. Feuerbach simply wanted to view this power naturalistically, rather than spiritually. Hence, he made it the distinguishing feature of the species. For Feuerbach, humanity is a 'generic-being' because it a special type of natural being which takes the genus (the universal) – and hence also its own species-character – as the object of both its thought and activity. This gave Feuerbach a naturalistic explanation of religion as a form of spiritual alienation. For him, religion was the illusory projection of the universal power of the human species onto an imaginary, supernatural being.

As we saw in the previous chapter, for Marx, labour was *the* distinctively human activity. Thus, rather than treating what Feuerbach called 'generic-being' naturalistically, Marx viewed it socially, as both the outcome and the means of the interchange between humans and the rest of nature. (Marx's critique of Feuerbach in 'On Feuerbach' is already implicit here, the previous year.) In Marx, labour appears as the practical source of human universality: 'that universality which makes the whole of nature its *inorganic* body'. Labour is a form of universality here in two respects. First, it treats nature – in principle, the whole of nature – as the 'direct means of life'. There is no limit, in advance, to those parts of nature off which humans might subsist. Second, in labouring, humanity treats nature as 'the matter, the object, and the instrument' of its own life activity. (Science is the intellectual form of this life activity, the developmental site of humanity's 'spiritual' generic-powers.) For Marx, humans are involved in a quasi-metabolic interaction with nature. Their universality does not precede this interaction, but is its result. Humanity is thus as universal as the objects of its activities. Human universality is a historical process based in human practices. The human is in a constant state of becoming *more* than what it was before. This is summed up in the idea of humanity as 'the living genus'.

Furthermore, this interaction with nature is so close, so existentially intimate, that nature is a kind of 'inorganic' extension of the human body. In labour, nature is a human prosthesis. With this idea, Marx anticipated recent debates about humans using technology to become cyborgs. The machines through which we relate to nature are as much a part of our bodies as our flesh, which consequently appears as merely a type of 'wetware'. The concept of labour as social production leads to a radically expanded conception of the human, which incorporates the whole of nature as humanity's 'inorganic body'. In being estranged from our own activity, we are also estranged from these more extended forms of the human that our work involves.

Finally, having articulated the relations between workers' alienation from their products, their life activity, and their generic-being, Marx reasoned that we are therefore also, at the same time, alienated from each other. This is a direct result of our alienation (as workers) from our activity, since this activity is the activity of *social* production. In being alienated from our activity, we are alienated from our own sociality, that is, from all the possible ways of freely being with others that are opened up by participation in a labouring collective. We become merely private individuals, whose contribution to social production is experienced merely as a 'means of individual existence'. The privatization of social life, so familiar in capitalist societies, is here traced back to private property itself.

Marx presented us with four, integrally related forms of alienation, all of which derive from the most basic features of waged work, and all of which remain prevalent today – indeed, far more so than in Marx's time. This is an astonishing, virtuoso theoretical performance, at once diagnostic, critical and explanatory. As Marx's subsequent study of political economy deepened, so too did the theoretical forms of his critique – especially, in *Capital*, in its development of the concept of 'value'. But Marx never entirely cast off the philosophical form of his first critique, in which he elaborated a new concept of the human. In this respect, it is not 'historical materialism' that is the driving force of Marx's intellectual project (let alone 'economics'), but the 'critique of political economy'. The first book to come out of Marx's study of political economy, in 1859, was entitled *A Contribution to a Critique of Political Economy* and *Capital* itself is subtitled *A Critique of Political Economy*. In this respect, strictly speaking, for Marx, there was no science of economics, but only critique.

5

THE CARNIVAL OF PHILOSOPHY

As in the history of philosophy there are nodal points which raise philosophy in itself to concretion, apprehend abstract principle in a totality, and thus break off the rectilinear process, so also there are moments when philosophy turns its eyes to the external world, and no longer apprehends it, but, as a practical person, weaves, as it were, intrigues with the world, emerges from the transparent kingdom of Amenthes and throws itself on the breast of the worldly Siren. That is the carnival of philosophy, whether it disguises itself as a dog like the Cynic, in priestly vestments like the Alexandrian, or in fragrant spring array like the Epicurean. It is essential that philosophy should then wear character masks. As Deucalion, according to the legend, cast stones behind him in creating human beings, so philosophy casts its regard behind it (the bones of its mother are luminous eyes) when its heart is set on creating a world. But as Prometheus, having stolen fire from heaven, begins to build houses and to settle upon the earth, so philosophy, expanded to be the whole world, turns against the world of appearance. The same now with the philosophy of Hegel.

Extract from 'Sixth Notebook',
Notebooks on Epicurean Philosophy, 1839

This chapter considers the development of Marx's early views about criticism as a realization of philosophy, from 'carnival' (1839), in the extract above, to revolution (1843), in the extract below:

However, a major difficulty appears to stand in the way of a *radical* German revolution.

For revolutions need a *passive* element, a *material* basis. Theory is actualized in a people only in so far as it is an actualization of the people's need. But will the enormous gap between the demands of German thought and the answers of German actuality be matched by a corresponding gap between civil society and the state and between civil society and itself? Will the theoretical needs be immediate practical needs? It is not enough for thought to strive for actualization, actuality must itself strive towards thought. . . .

So where is the *positive* possibility of a German emancipation?

Answer: in the formation of a class with radical chains, a class of civil society which is not a class of civil society, an estate [*Stand*] which is the dissolution of all estates, a sphere which has a universal character because of its universal suffering and claims no *particular right* because no *particular wrong* but wrong generally is perpetrated against it; which can no longer claim a *historical* but only a *human* title; which does not stand in one-sided opposition to the consequences but in all-sided opposition to the premises of the German state; a sphere, finally, which cannot emancipate itself without emancipating itself from – and thereby emancipating – all other spheres of society, which is, in a word, the *complete loss* of humanity and which can therefore win itself only through the *complete rewinning of humanity.* This dissolution of society as a particular estate is the *proletariat.*

The proletariat is coming into being in Germany only as a result of the emergent *industrial* movement . . .

By proclaiming the *dissolution of the previously existing world order* the proletariat merely states the secret of its own existence, for it is *in fact* the dissolution of that world order. By demanding the *negation of private property*, the proletariat merely raises to the rank of a *principle of society* what society has made *its* [the proletariat's] principle, what, without its consent, is already embodied in *it* as the negative result of society . . .

As philosophy finds its *material* weapons in the proletariat, so the proletariat finds its *spiritual* weapons in philosophy. And once the lightning of thought has struck deeply into this ingenuous soil of the people, emancipation will transform the *Germans* into *human beings*. . . .

The *head* of this emancipation is *philosophy*, its *heart* is the *proletariat*. Philosophy cannot actualize itself without the supersession of the proletariat, the proletariat cannot supersede itself without the actualization of philosophy.

Extract from 'Contribution to Critique of Hegel's
Philosophy of Right: Introduction', 1843/4

All of Marx's writings are bound up with the notion of criticism or critique. In this respect, Marx stands within the Kantian tradition of the German Enlightenment. In his *Critique of Pure Reason* (1781), Kant wrote: 'Our age is the genuine age of *criticism*, to which everything must submit . . . there is nothing so important because of its utility, nothing so holy, that it may be exempted from this searching review and inspection, which knows no respect for persons.'[15] Similarly, in a letter outlining his plans for a new journal in the autumn of 1843, Marx wrote: 'It is all the more clear what we have to accomplish at present: . . . *ruthless criticism of all that exists*, ruthless both in the sense of not being afraid of the results it arrives at and in the sense of being just as little afraid of conflict with the powers that be'(*MECW* 1, 144). For the young Marx, such criticism was the means by which philosophy was to become practical and hence 'real'. However, while Marx's notion of critique was based in the Enlightenment, it was nonetheless somewhat different from Kant's, since it developed within the more historical philosophy of Hegelianism.

For both Kant and Hegel, the criterion of criticism was 'reason'. But they had different ideas about what reason was. For Kant, reason was an autonomous human faculty with 'eternal and unchangeable laws'. It possessed the theoretical power to establish a certain limited number of truths, independently of experience. Philosophically, criticism involved the application of reason to establish the boundaries of its (reason's) own legitimacy. Critique, in other words, was first and foremost criticism of reason by reason. It had a Socratic dimension, it was the *self-knowledge* of reason. The practical implementation of the demands of reason – for example, free speech – was, however, for Kant, a more complicated issue, since it depended upon a certain public 'maturity'.[16]

For Hegel, on the other hand, reason was a power inherent in history. Reason was not merely a human faculty, it was the intelligible aspect of reality itself. Famously, in the preface to his *Philosophy of Right* (1821), Hegel wrote: 'What is rational is actual and what is actual is rational.' Hegel denied actuality to the irrational or the unintelligible. For him the irrational may *exist*, but it is not 'actual', in the sense that it does not partake in the movement of history; it is mere contingency. This is a difficult but crucial distinction. Reality (*Realität*), for Hegel, was made up of a combination of actuality (*Wirklichkeit*) and the merely existing or contingent. Philosophy's task was to grasp what is rational, and hence actual, *within* the real. The ultimate criterion of historical judgement was the complete actualization of reason. Hegel called this the 'idea'. It is equivalent to the realization of freedom and hence the end of history as a process of development. This idea was revived and popularized in the 1990s, as an achievement of US capitalism, by Francis Fukuyama.[17]

Applying the distinction between 'reality' and 'actuality' to history allowed Hegel to view history as the process of reason becoming actual. At any particular moment in world-history, within this scenario, reason could be judged to have reached a certain stage of development, demonstrable in the rationality embodied in its social institutions (Hegel called this 'objective spirit'). Within this scenario, critique was (in Marx's words) the 'measurement of the particular actuality by the idea' (*MECW* 1, 85).

When the young Marx arrived at Berlin University to study law in October 1836, at the age of eighteen, Hegel had been dead for less than five years. And while the power of the Hegelian School within the Prussian academic establishment had begun to wane in the wake of the political reaction of 1832–4, its influence remained pervasive. The first edition of Hegel's collected works was in the process of being published. Eduard Gans, whose lectures on law Marx would attend, was editing Hegel's *Lectures on the Philosophy of History*, which appeared the following year (1837). It was thus hardly surprising that, as Marx developed what he described in a letter to his father as 'an urge to wrestle with philosophy', it should have been Hegel's philosophy with which he would wrestle.

At first, Marx was repelled by what he called 'the grotesque craggy melody' of Hegel's system, the baroque formalism of a self-sufficient system, distanced from life. Yet, in the spirit of

Romanticism, he nonetheless sought a systematic perspective from which to organize the materials of his legal studies. Having attempted, and failed, to create one himself (written in the form of a philosophical dialogue between art and science), he found himself delivered up 'into the arms of the enemy' (*MECW* 1, 10–21). That enemy was at once Hegel and philosophy itself. Hegelian philosophy was an enemy to Marx's poetic aspirations, but it was also an enemy to his father's more instrumental aspirations for his son's legal career. In so far as philosophy was an enemy to the constrictions of parental ambition, this particular enemy became his friend.

After Hegel's death in 1833, the Hegelian School of philosophers split into two factions, representing competing political judgements. The conservative, right-wing or orthodox Hegelians judged that the existing institutions of Prussian society were indeed sufficiently rational to represent the self-actualization of the idea. They therefore supported them politically. The radical, left-wing or critical Hegelians, on the other hand, judged that existing institutions failed to live up to Hegel's conception of their ideal rational form. They therefore criticized them as irrational. This criticism intensified in 1840 when Friedrich Wilhelm IV ascended to the throne in Prussia and instituted a harsh regime of state censorship. This regime thwarted Marx's plans for an academic post and subsequently led to the closure of the newspaper that he was editing, the *Rhenish Times.* For a period (1840–4), Marx was one of a new, more politically radical generation of Left Hegelians known as the Young Hegelians.

The extracts for this chapter are taken from the beginning and the end of this period. The first one outlines Marx's conception of the historical demand that philosophy should become political after Hegel – and indicates Marx's unique awareness of the contradictions of this process. The second sets out Marx's provisional solution to the problem of how philosophy, having become 'immediately' political, as 'criticism of all that exists', might make changes to the social world.

The *Notebooks on Epicurean Philosophy* contain the notes from Marx's doctoral research. The ostensible topic of this dissertation was 'The Difference between the Democritean and Epicurean Philosophy of Nature' – an apparent backwater in the history of ancient Greek thought. However, Marx's philosophical agenda was a contemporary one: namely, how could philosophy continue to progress after a 'total' philosophy such as Hegel's? The link was an analogy between the historical situation of Hegel's philosophy and that of Aristotle's. Marx sought a solution to the problem of philosophy after Hegel by looking back at what happened in Greek philosophy after Aristotle. For Marx, Aristotle and Hegel represent 'nodal points' at which philosophy became 'concrete' by having 'apprehended abstract principles in a totality' – that is, by providing a systematic account of the interconnections between the elements of knowledge as a whole. Each philosophy was an interruption in philosophy's normal historical development, in so far as it is assumed that philosophy moves forward by particular principles being developed in a piecemeal fashion.

In itself, this analogy was by no means original, since Hegel had thought of himself as – as indeed he was – a modern-day Aristotle. Aristotle's summary of previous Greek philosophy in book one of his *Metaphysics* was the model for Hegel's history of philosophy. What was original was Marx's extension of this parallel to his own day, as a diagnostic tool for exploring how philosophy could continue *after* Hegel.

What happened after Aristotle, Marx argued, was that philosophy, 'expanded to be the whole world' (i.e. mirroring the world as a whole in thought) 'turn[ed] against the world of appearance'. No longer content with just knowing the world – complete in thought, but frustrated by its restriction to thought – philosophy becomes 'a practical person' and 'weaves intrigues with the world'. It succumbs to the temptation of the Sirens, who call to it to emerge from its shadowy existence as pure thought and join the human world. (The kingdom of Amenthes was the mythical Egyptian version of Hades, where souls go after death.) What philosophy wants to do at such moments, Marx is suggesting, is to heal the gap between itself and the world, by recreating the world in its own image. Its project is to *realize itself*, to make itself real. For Marx at this point, the means for such a realization was critique. Critique was an '*immediate* realization of philosophy' (*MECW* 1, 85).

Clearly, this is both a philosophically idealist and a politically idealistic project. It sets out an ideal and demands that the world adjust itself to it. It is striking, for example, to find Marx writing in October 1842 of the superior power of ideas over mass politics:

> We are firmly convinced that the real *danger* lies not in *practical attempts*, but in the *theoretical elaboration* of communist ideas, for practical attempts, even *mass attempts*, can be answered by *cannon* as soon as they become dangerous, whereas *ideas*, which have conquered our intellect and taken possession of our minds, ideas to which reason has fettered our conscience, are chains from which one cannot free oneself without a broken heart; they are demons which human beings can vanquish only by submitting to them. (*MECW* 1, 220–21)

The practical medium for such purely ideological conflict was journalism. Marx conceived of journalism as 'worldly philosophy'. Nonetheless, for all his optimism about the power of ideas, at this time, Marx was well aware of the subjectively one-sided character of this Enlightenment conception of critique. If reason was different from and opposed to the world, there must be some inadequacy or limitation in reason itself, as well as in the world – that is, it must be a merely subjective conception of reason that opposes itself to the world. But Marx thought this inevitable in the wake of a 'total' philosophy like Hegel's.

There are several reasons why Marx described these moments in the wake of total philosophies as carnivals. First, they are periodic interruptions in the normal course of philosophical development, just as carnivals are interruptions of everyday life. Second, like carnivals, they involve liberation from authority (in these cases, the philosophical authorities of Aristotle and Hegel). Finally, in becoming practical, in intervening in the social world, total philosophies are forced to take sides, to identify with one particular party in on-going social conflicts, and hence to wear the 'mask' of a particular social character. Like carnival masks, these critical-philosophical masks are distorted or inverted images of authority (the authority of philosophy). Philosophy, which aspires to be universal, thus appears within the real only in the guise of particular characters. This is its fundamental contradiction at such times.

Marx's first example is the Cynic Diogenes through whom philosophy appears as a dog. (The word 'cynic' stems from the Greek word '*kūon*', meaning 'dog'. Diogenes, the first Cynic, was nicknamed '*Kūon*' because he masturbated publicly, in the market place, in order to make the philosophical point that human happiness is attained through the satisfaction of the simplest natural needs.) Marx recognized that when philosophy becomes particular in this way the realization of philosophy in the actual world 'is also its *loss*' (*MECW* 1, 87) – the loss of its *absolute* universality by the reduction of this universality to a subjective, and hence one-sided form. It is interesting that Marx expressed all this in such a maniacally mythological metaphorical manner. His whole depiction of Hegelianism as a total philosophy becoming practical and one-sided is a Romantic one, not simply in literary terms, but philosophically too. It displays a Romantic awareness of the contradiction inherent in the very idea of a systematic or 'total' philosophy.

The image of the mask is more often associated with Nietzsche than with Marx, but it recurs throughout Marx's writings, most notably in the opening to *The 18th Brumaire of Louis Bonapa*rte (1852). There masks appear as part of a 'process of world-historical necromancy', in which:

> Luther put on the mask of the apostle Paul; the Revolution
> of 1789–1814 draped itself alternately as the Roman
> republic and the Roman empire; and the revolution of
> 1848 knew no better than to parody at some points 1789
> and at others the revolutionary traditions of 1793–5.

In 1852, masks are presented as means of historical borrowings that register a weakness in the revolutionary imaginary, a 'superstitious regard for the past, a mode of repetition that returns tragedy as farce' (*MECW* 11, 103–4). This is because, by then, Marx believed he had solved the problem of philosophy's worldly representation (the gap between the universality of philosophy and the particularities of the social world), without recourse to masks. This is the role of the proletariat in the second extract. Or, we might wonder, will the proletariat, in fact, turn out to be philosophy's ultimate mask?

Marx's 'Introduction' to his unfinished 'Contribution to a Critique of Hegel's Philosophy of Right' is an extraordinary text. Written at the beginning of his stay in Paris in late autumn, early winter 1843–4, it both sums up his thought and moves decisively beyond anything he had previously written, in a number of startling and often contradictory ways. In this respect, it is very much a nodal point in his own development. Drawing upon his recent studies in political history (the *Kreuznach Notebooks*, May–October 1843), and in the first flush of his encounter with German émigré socialist organizations in Paris, Marx fused the contradictory strands of his earlier writings into a tense, aphoristic, pre-emptive unity that abounds with new contradictions and directions for thought. At once more historically specific than Marx's previous theoretical writings (in its focus on the peculiarities of Prussia as an underdeveloped European state), it is nonetheless, in its concluding political triumphancy, also one of the most speculative and over-reaching – prophetic and almost ecstatic – of his texts.

Surprisingly, given that it is such a political text, the 'Introduction' involves a systematic rethinking of the passage from the *Notebooks on Epicurean Philosophy* about how philosophy might be realized. This is a good example of the way in which the unity of Marx's thought derives, in part, from his constant reworking of earlier unpublished texts. The more thoroughly one excavates the textual detail of Marx's writings, the clearer it becomes that he was involved in a constant dialogue with himself – returning to old manuscripts and notebooks, not only for inspiration and reference, but as a source of images and phrases, textual matter itself. The first version of the idea provided Marx with his conception of journalistic criticism as 'worldly philosophy'. The new version provides a theoretical basis for his politics. The realization of philosophy now requires the self-abolition of the proletariat: an act through which, in emancipating itself, the proletariat simultaneously abolishes itself as a class. This new conception is characterized by a radical deflation in the practical claims made on behalf of intellectual criticism. Conditions in Germany, Marx now argued, are 'below the level of history' and as such 'beneath any criticism': 'Criticism no longer appears as an *end in itself*, but only as a *means*. Its essential sentiment is *indignation*, its essential activity is *denunciation*' (*MECW* 3, 177). Philosophy cannot be realized by criticism alone. Marx's focus switched to those elements of actuality that 'strive towards thought', towards reason, which, in the tradition of the German Enlightenment, he continued to understand as the basis of freedom.

Marx found these elements in the proletariat, *not* because they are the labouring class (a quite different argument that he will use later, elsewhere), but because they are the *excluded* class, the class without property and, indeed, without political representation in Germany at that time. The use of the term 'proletariat' for the lowest social class derives from ancient Rome. Proletarians were citizens of Rome who were regarded as contributing nothing to the state except their offspring. (The word comes from the Latin *proles*, offspring). The idea was taken up into modern politics in the pre-revolutionary context of mid-eighteenth-century France, with which Marx's recent studies in political history had familiarized him. In transposing it into the German context, Marx radically expanded the proletariat's purported social and political role.

The extract argues for the political radicalism and utopian potential of the socially excluded, for whom the proletariat functions as both the emblem and the embodiment. Its argument has had a political influence far beyond the confines of the working-class politics with which Marxism became associated: in feminism, anti-colonialism, the black civil rights movement, anti-psychiatry, prisoners' organizations, indigenous movements – throughout the radical Left movements of the second half of the twentieth century, in fact. Each of these movements made political claims on the basis of the universal significance of their exclusion from social recognition of one kind or another.

It was the economic and political underdevelopment of Germany that made the proletariat there, for Marx, 'a class with radical chains'. It is symptomatic of this underdevelopment that, in describing the proletariat, Marx oscillated between the modern (economic) concept of class and the feudal (political) concept of estate. In describing the contradictory position of the proletariat in Germany, Marx calls it both 'a class of civil society which is not a class of civil society' and 'an estate which is the dissolution of all estates'. It is a class of civil society (*die bürgerliche Gesellschaft* – literally, 'bourgeois' society) because it is an essential part of the capitalist economy. It is *not* a class of civil society in so far as civil society exceeds the economy, and includes both the administration of justice (property law) and the political representation of economic interests, from which the proletariat was excluded.

The German proletariat was 'an estate which is the dissolution of all estates' because, for Marx, it was a *particular* social force (an estate) that embodies a *universal* interest (hence an end to the distinction between estates) by virtue of its embodiment of the principle of exclusion. As such, the German proletariat was an incarnation of suffering, an embodiment of a universal humanity in a negative guise. In Germany in 1843, for Marx, this made the proletariat the potential material carrier (or 'heart') of philosophical reason. Philosophy and the proletariat are presented as opposed but complementary forms of universality: ideal and material, respectively. And just as the proletariat promises to provide philosophy with the material force lacked by criticism, so philosophy promises to provide the proletariat with consciousness of its own universality. For philosophy to be actualized, the proletariat must transform its negative universality (suffering) into a new positive form of humanity, through consciousness of its historical role. At this point, Marx described this as emancipation. Soon, it will become communism.

Within this discourse, philosophy and the proletariat are ultimately no less allegorical figures than the mythological characters in the extract from the doctoral notebooks. But if the revolution Marx foresaw here is another carnival of philosophy, it will be one at which, at the crucial moment, one of the participants rips off all of the masks, bringing the carnival to an end by revealing the common humanity beneath each.

6

COMMUNISM

> ... the theory of the communists can be summed up in the
> single sentence: supersession of private property.
>
> Karl Marx and Friedrich Engels,
> *Manifesto of the Communist Party*, 1848

But the opposition between *propertylessness* and *property*
is still an indifferent opposition, not grasped in its *active
connection*, its *inner* relation, not yet grasped as *contradiction*, as long as it is not understood as the antithesis
between *labour* and *capital* ... labour, the subjective
essence of private property as exclusion of property, and
capital, objective labour as exclusion of labour, constitute
private property in its developed relation of contradiction: a
vigorous relation, therefore, driving towards resolution. . . .

In grasping this relation in its *generality*, communism is
(1) in its initial form only a *generalization* and completion
of that relation ... the domination of *material* property
bulks so large that it threatens to destroy everything which
is not capable of being possessed by everyone as *private
property*. Physical, immediate *possession* is the only
purpose of life and existence for it; the category of the

worker is not superseded but extended to all humankind; it wants to abstract from talent, etc, in a *violent* manner.

The relation of private property remains the relation of the community to the world of things; ultimately this movement to oppose general private property to private property is expressed in the bestial form of opposing to marriage (which is admittedly a *form* of *exclusive private property*) the community of women, in which the woman becomes *communal* and *common* property. One might say that this thought of the *community of women* is the *revealed secret* of this as yet wholly crude and unthinking communism. Just as women are to go from marriage into general prostitution, so the whole world of wealth (i.e. the objective essence of humankind) is to make the transition from the relation of exclusive marriage with the private owner to relation of universal prostitution with the community. This communism, in so far as it negates the personalities of men and women in every sphere, is but the consistent expression of private property, which this negation is. General *envy* constituting itself as a power is the hidden form in which *greed* reasserts itself and satisfies itself, but in *another* way . . . The crude communist is merely the culmination of this envy and desire to level down on the basis of a *preconceived* minimum. It has a *definite, limited* measure. How little this abolition of private property is an actual appropriation is shown by the abstract negation of the entire world of culture and civilization, and the return to the *unnatural* simplicity of the *poor* men and women who have no needs, who have not even reached the stage of private property, let alone gone beyond it. . . .

The first positive abolition of private property – *crude* communism – is therefore only a *form of appearance* of the vileness of private property, which wants to set itself up as the *positive community*.

(2) Communism (a) still of a political nature, democratic or despotic; (b) with the abolition of the state, but still essentially incomplete and influenced by private property, i.e., the estrangement of humankind. In both forms communism already knows itself as the reintegration or return of humankind into itself, the supersession of humankind's self-estrangement; but since it has not yet comprehended the positive essence of private property or understood the *human* nature of need, it is still held captive and contaminated by private property. It has understood its concept, but not yet its essence.

(3) *Communism* as the *positive* supersession of *private property* as *human self-estrangement*, and hence the actual *appropriation of the human* essence by and for humankind; hence as the complete return of humankind to itself as a *social*, i.e. human humankind, a return which has become conscious and takes place within the entire wealth of the previous development. This communism, as fully developed naturalism = humanism, and as fully developed humanism = naturalism; it is the *genuine* resolution of the conflict between humankind and nature, and within humankind, the true resolution of the conflict between existence and essence, between objectification and self-affirmation, between freedom and necessity, between individual and species. It is the riddle of history solved and it knows itself to be this solution.

Extract from *Economic and
Philosophical Manuscripts*, 1844

Communism is the central political idea of Marx's thought. It is not a narrowly political idea, but a social conception with a philosophical and historical meaning. In fact, one way that Marx and Engels distinguished communists from other Left groups was by communists' recognition of 'the insufficiency of merely political revolutions' and 'the necessity of a total social change' (Engels, Preface to the 1888 English edition of the *Communist Manifesto*, *MECW* 26, 515). To understand Marx's concept of communism, we must thus start from its philosophical core, discern its historical meaning, and thereby, finally, arrive at its more concrete political significance.

The political meaning of Marx's thought has often been obscured by its association with the actually existing state socialism of the Soviet Union, and the politics of the international communist movement more generally, in the period following the Second World War.[18] Once 'Marxism–Leninism' became the official ideology of the mainstream of that movement, there was an inevitable tendency for Marx's views about communism to become confused with the principles and policies of those parties that called themselves 'communist'. Yet Marx's conception of communism was not primarily that of a particular type of political party, let alone a state, but of a society without class antagonisms, without classes: 'an association in which the free development of each is the condition of the free development of all', as the *Communist Manifesto* puts it. In this respect it is the polar opposite of alienation, discussed in chapter four. Communism is a de-alienated society. As we have seen, Marx understood alienation to derive from 'the fact of private property'. The key to the idea of communism is the negation of private property.

Two things require clarification: what Marx meant by 'private property' and what is involved in constructing a concept of something (communism) as the 'negation' of something else (private property). An explanation of the latter will require a brief digression into the tricky subject of dialectics. In particular, we need to understand the dialectical category of supersession, since Marx's conception of communism is of it as a supersession of private property.

Private property is easier to understand than dialectical logic, yet it is a little more complicated than might be supposed. As Marx makes clear, it is not property in general which is the issue. There are no property relations 'in general', but only historically specific social forms of property. It is *private* property in the bourgeois sense of *exclusive* and hence *alienable* rights of ownership that is at issue – something quite different from feudal property, for example, which was not alienable (could not be sold), but was held on behalf of future generations and bestowed certain rights on its current 'owner'. Nor was Marx concerned with the ownership of everyday items of personal use. It is the ownership of means of production, and hence the mode of access to means of subsistence, that occupied him, since this is what determines the distribution of social power and thereby the fundamental character of a society. This is why Marx thought that the antithesis between 'propertylessness and property' in general is 'indifferent'. When applied to capitalist societies, it conceals rather than reveals the true antithesis, which is between labour and capital.

Marx's prose in the *Economic and Philosophical Manuscripts* is highly condensed and needs some unpacking. By 'labour' Marx meant the class of wage-labourers, the vast majority of the population in capitalist societies. But labour is not *wholly* propertyless. It has property in itself, its capacity to labour, as well as in everyday items of consumption needed to reproduce its labour-power. In this latter respect, nowadays in Western capitalist societies, this will often include a house, for example. Private property *looks* as if it is a generalized condition, where some people simply have more than others. It *looks* as if inequality is a purely quantitative phenomenon, a question of

'how much' property different people have, expressed in
money, the universal equivalent. However, Marx thought that
this way of looking at things conceals a more fundamental,
qualitative difference, the division of society into classes on the
basis of *what* people own: on the one hand, labour-power
and items of consumption (the worker), and on the other, the
means of production and hence also its products (capital). For
Marx, the true social, political – and, one might add, existential – meaning of private property is to be found in this social
division, which is internal to the legal form of private property itself.

From this point of view, Marx argued, the restricted form
of private property characteristic of labour (ownership of
labour-power and items of consumption) is actually an expression of the *exclusion* of labourers from ownership in *other*
means of production. Hence, Marx's polemical and paradoxical formulation: labour is 'private property as exclusion of
property'. The private property of labour involves a specific
form of propertylessness. This is especially paradoxical since,
in Marx's view, labour is the 'subjective essence' of private
property. He is referring here to the fact it is the activity of
labouring that produces what is bought and sold – whether
they be goods or services.

On the other hand, Marx referred to capital as 'objective
labour' because the means of production (raw materials,
machines, buildings, etc) that are brought together in the production process are the products of past production: hence,
'objectifications of labour' or 'objective labour'. Yet, by definition, labour is excluded from ownership of capital. So, capital
as objective (or as Marx would later say, 'dead') labour is an
'exclusion' of (what Marx would later call 'living') labour.

Marx's penchant for dense, elliptical and paradoxical
formulations here is not just a rhetorical and an aesthetic

conceit – though it is also those things. It is a form of conceptual reduction. He boils down an idea to its most basic elements and examines their relations to one another, from the standpoint of their mutual dependence. This is a process of analysis that reveals concepts to be both internally complex and dynamic entities. In this case, the claim is that private property – an apparently straightforward legal form – actually contains a contradictory relation between two social elements, labour and capital, each of which itself has an internally contradictory structure. Under the pressure of such an examination, concepts can be made to dance. It takes hard work to reconstruct the choreography from the performance. But it is important to recognize that these are not just powerful and difficult phrases, they are highly condensed arguments.

The next step in Marx's argument distinguishes three different conceptions of communism, based on three different ways of 'negating' private property. It is only the third of these that Marx accepted as philosophically adequate. The other two, he argued, are inadequate conceptions because they are based on inadequate concepts of private property. The things they negate are only partially understood. The conception of negation at play here is a dialectical one. It understands concepts to be 'internally' related to one another in their meanings; and it takes these relations to be relations of either identity or difference. A difference in meaning is understood logically as a 'negation'. For example, take the conceptual pair: property and propertylessness. Propertylessness or lack of property is a negation of property (formally, it is simply not-property). But this negation is internal to the concept of property in so far as what is not property (a potentially infinite set) is defined exclusively, albeit negatively, in terms of property itself. This is why Marx called the antithesis an indifferent one. The negation of property by propertylessness (practically, the moral act of giving up ownership – asceticism, for example) has no progressive political content for Marx since it leaves the institution of property intact. It will be either a solely individual act or a universal impoverishment, since no alterative system of production and distribution of goods to the existing one is proposed. What Marx called 'crude communism' makes the converse error: it describes a situation in which private property is generalized, to everyone, collectively.

The political virtue of the extract above is the explicitness with which it expresses Marx's opposition to 'crude communism'. His opposition has two main planks, opposition to crude communism's reduction of what is held socially in common to a form of private ownership; and its associated failure to recognize the historical character of human needs. As a result, crude communism both puts into common ownership things that are not appropriately owned at all – the community of women as universal prostitution was Marx's powerful example – and it 'negates the personalities' of men and women by reducing objects of ownership to the lowest common dominator in order that everyone can share in them. This results in what Marx called 'an abstract negation of the entire world of culture and civilization'. This sounds familiar, it is the popular stereotype of communism as a general social-levelling, of which Marxism has often been falsely accused by its enemies. Yet for Marx this would not be emancipation, but the culmination of envy, a type of resentment. From Marx's point of view, it is not really communism at all, but a version of 'the vileness of private property' itself. The popular stereotype of communism is thus the precise opposite of Marx's view. For Marx and Engels: 'Communism deprives no one of the power to appropriate the products of society; all it does is deprive them of the power to subjugate the labour of others by means of such appropriation' (*MECW* 6, 500).

The reference to envy is interesting because it connects Marx's critique of crude communism to Nietzsche's analysis of Christianity as a slave morality based on resentment, in his *Genealogy of Morality* (1887). The radical egalitarianism of early Christianity, one can say, was a type of crude communism. It made political sense at that time, when human needs were still relatively simple. In relation to capitalism, however, crude communism represents a historical regression – a de-humanization, in fact. An adequate conception of communism, on the other hand, Marx claimed, will locate communism '*within* the entire wealth of the previous development'. That is to say, it will exclude nothing of what has been progressive in history up to this point. It will take the productivity of capitalism as its condition. This is communism as 'the positive supersession of private property as human self-estrangement and hence the actual appropriation of the human essence by and for humankind'. Only if private property is grasped in its most fundamental character as 'human self-estrangement', Marx is arguing, can its negation result in a genuine emancipation.

Marx used two concepts that were central to Hegel's philosophy to theorize the transition from capitalism to communism: supersession and appropriation. Supersession (or 'sublation' as the German *Aufhebung* is sometimes translated) is the term used in dialectical logic to describe the relationship of a new stage of development to the one that precedes it. It has three main senses, all of which were used by Hegel: (i) to raise or lift up; (ii) to annul, abolish, destroy, cancel or suspend; (iii) to save or preserve. Dialectical supersession is a process that lifts something to a higher power by cancelling or abolishing it in its existing form while nonetheless preserving something about it within its new form. Appropriation is the term used by Hegel to describe the process whereby something that has been alienated (externalized and thereby estranged) is recovered or repossessed. If alienation is a negation of the human, appropriation is a 'negation of the negation' and hence a certain kind of return. The negation of private property as human self-estrangement will be a supersession of private property only if it is also an appropriation – an appropriation of the previously alienated essence of the human.

We are now in a position to understand what Marx meant by communism as the 'positive supersession of private property as human self-estrangement'. It means that communism abolishes private property in such a way as to move humanity to a more advanced stage of historical development because it nonetheless preserves those things about the system of private property that contributed to human development – namely, the 'human' content of its productive power and its generation of new needs, which was alienated within the system of private property itself. (The term 'positive' was used by Marx to denote that this is to be an actual material process, rather than merely a movement in thought; it is used to distinguish Marx's dialectic from Hegel's.) This supersession is an appropriation because it will return to men and women something from which they were previously estranged: namely, their life-activity, its products, their generic-being, and their relations to one another – the four types of alienation produced by private property discussed in chapter four. As such, Marx claims, communism will resolve the conflict between humankind and nature. This is an extraordinary, utopian speculative claim. It means that communism will not be a stage of historical development in any usual sense, since no further 'development' will come after it, much like Hegel's end of history. This is why Marx called it 'the riddle of history solved'. It will inaugurate a new kind of time, the time of human freedom. It will be the beginning of a new kind of 'history': the history of freedom.

The most important thing, politically, in this conception is the element of preservation in the supersession of private property. What Marx understood as communism would abolish private property – it would be a system of common ownership of the means of production – but it would not regress behind the enormous historical advance for the species represented by capitalism. It is this historical dimension that distinguishes Marx's conception of communism from previous ones, which were utopian, such as the early nineteenth-century communisms of Charles Fourier and Robert Owen. To differentiate his communism more sharply from these, Marx came to place less emphasis on communism as a theoretical idea (in case it be taken for 'an *ideal* to which reality will have to adjust itself') and more emphasis on its immanence to history. In *The German Ideology*, for example, communism is described as 'the *real* movement that abolishes the present state of things' (*MECW* 5, 49). Marx's and Engels's conception of a communist party was the political representative of the general historical movement of the supersession of private property. However, the historical possibility of communism is based on the revolutionary role that *capitalism* plays in developing the forces of production.

7

CAPITALISM AS MODERNITY

The history of all hitherto existing society is the history of class struggle . . .

The bourgeoisie, historically, has played a most revolutionary part. . . .

The bourgeoisie cannot exist without constantly revolutionizing the instruments of production, and thereby the relations of production, and with them the whole relations of society. Conservation of the old modes of production in unaltered form, was, on the contrary, the first condition of existence for all earlier industrial classes. Constant revolutionizing of production, uninterrupted disturbance of all social conditions, everlasting uncertainty and agitation distinguish the bourgeois epoch from all earlier ones. All fixed, fast-frozen relations, with their train of ancient and venerable prejudices and opinions, are swept away, all new-formed ones become antiquated before they can ossify. All that is solid melts into air, all that is holy is profaned, and men and women are at last compelled to face with sober senses their real conditions of life, and relations with their kind.

The need for a constantly expanding market for its products chases the bourgeoisie over the whole surface of the globe. It must nestle everywhere, settle everywhere, establish connections everywhere.

The bourgeoisie has through its exploitation of the world market given a cosmopolitan character to production and consumption in every country. To the great chargin of reactionaries, it has drawn from under the feet of industry the national ground on which it stood. They are dislodged by new industries, whose introduction becomes a life and death question for all civilized nations, by industries that no longer work up indigenous raw material, but raw material drawn from the remotest zones; industries whose products are consumed, not only at home, but in every corner of the globe. In place of the old wants, satisfied by the productions of the country, we find new wants, requiring for their satisfaction the products of distant lands and climes. In place of the old local and national seclusion and self-sufficiency, we have intercourse in every direction, all-round interdependence of nations. And as in material, so also in intellectual production. The intellectual creations of individual nations become common property. National one-sidedness and narrow-mindedness become more and more impossible, and from the numerous national and local literatures there arises a world literature.

The bourgeoisie, by the rapid improvement of all instruments of production, by the immensely facilitated means of communication, draws all, even the most barbarian, nations into civilization. The cheap prices of its commodities are the heavy artillery with which it batters down all Chinese walls, with which it forces the barbarians' intensely obstinate hatred of foreigners to capitulate. It compels all nations, on pain of extinction, to adopt the bourgeois mode of production; it compels them to introduce so-called civilization into their midst, i.e. to become

bourgeois themselves. In one word, it creates a world after
its own image.

Extract from Marx/Engels, 'Bourgeois and Proletarians',
Manifesto of the Communist Party, 1848

The *Communist Manifesto* lays down the perspective, principles
and positions of the Communist League. The League was
founded in 1847 as a reorganization of the League of the Just,
a previously covert émigré German workers' organization set
up in Paris a decade earlier. The *Manifesto* commits the League
to 'the forcible overthrow of all existing social conditions'
through a communist revolution in which the fall of the bourgeoisie and the victory of the proletariat are declared 'equally
inevitable' (*MECW* 6, 519, 496).[19] However, as this extract
shows, the *Manifesto* also contains what the North American
libertarian Marshall Berman has described as 'a lyrical cele-
bration of bourgeois works'.[20] There is a striking depiction of
capitalism as a progressive (indeed, 'revolutionary') and globalizing world-historical force – progressive, in fact, in its very
globalizing function. It is hard to read this extract today without thinking of the extraordinary pace of the current capitalistic
transformation of China.

The progressive character of capitalism's revolutionizing of
all social relations is seen to lie primarily in its *destructiveness*.
But this destructiveness is not confined to capitalism's structural annihilation of social constraints such as religion, nation,
family, age, sex – important as this is. It is not a one-off act,
marking the onset of capitalism in any particular social space.
It extends to a destructiveness of capitalism towards itself.
Marx writes of capitalism's '*constant* revolutionizing of production', '*uninterrupted* disturbance of all social conditions',
'*everlasting* uncertainty and agitation', and the antiquation of
'*all new-formed* [relations] . . . before they can ossify [my

emphasis]'. This is a permanent maelstrom of change, a permanent revolution of destruction and creation generating the experience of modernity itself.

If modernity is the name for a particular experience of historical time, a restless temporal logic of negation that prioritizes the present over the past, and the future over the present – in a word, a logic of the *new*[21]– then, in Marx's depiction, capitalism is the production of modernity on a global scale. In celebrating the destructiveness of capitalism, Marx is celebrating the *creative* destructiveness of modernity. ('"Construction" presupposes "destruction"', as Walter Benjamin put it.)[22] Marx is celebrating capitalism *as* modernity, rather than in any of its other aspects; he is celebrating capitalism's creation of the *possibility* of that 'all-round development' that Marx identified with freedom. Furthermore, this breathless hymn to capitalism as modernity is not just part of the subject matter of the *Manifesto*, it is not just one side of a historical argument. It inhabits the *Manifesto*. One might say that it possesses it (in the sense of possession by spirits, possession by the devil), from its image of history right down to the rhythm of its prose.

However much the *Manifesto* may be an exhortation to the proletariat to abolish capitalism, this historical role is nonetheless presented as rigorously internal to the developmental logic of capitalism itself. The proletariat appears as a genie, who will succeed because 'modern bourgeois society . . . is like the sorcerer who is no longer able to control the powers of the nether world whom he has called up by his spells' (*MECW* 6, 489). These powers are the new productive forces unleashed by capitalism of which the proletariat is but the prospective historical representative. The destructive power of the proletariat – its purported ability to bring down the system of capitalism – is a deflection of the destructive power of capitalism itself. This is imprinted on the reader by the very tempo of the text. In its first section, 'Bourgeois and Proletarians', the bourgeoisie is the subject of almost every sentence. In mimicking the time of modernity (by the use of repetition, for example, to reproduce the metronomic time of the machine), the *Manifesto* is not just about modernity, and it is not just a modern text: it is a modernist text. It affirms the temporality of the new. (In its deepest sense, modernism cannot be defined merely stylistically; it is the cultural affirmation of a particular experience of time, the new.)[23]

To read the *Communist Manifesto* for its contemporary significance, we need to approach it as both a historical argument about the role of social classes as agents of historical change and an extraordinary literary achievement. At its grandest, it aims to produce a structure of experience within the reader equivalent to the experience of history itself. The power of the text derives from the connection between these two levels: its ability to present a historical argument imagistically. Its weakness lies in this same connection: in the conflation of theoretical terms that these images involve.

The first thing to note about the *Communist Manifesto*'s literary form is that it is the synthesis of a number of pre-existing, historically discrete literary forms, each of which can be traced in earlier texts and manuscript materials by Marx and Engels themselves: the catechism, the historical narrative, the Gothic tale, the political programme, the critique of political economy, and the literature review. Each of these literary forms functions as a separate compositional element of the *Manifesto*, while also producing meaning relationally, from its position within the whole. The *Manifesto*'s basic compositional procedure is thus a kind of montage. But what is the principle governing the montage, the principle that produces the unity of the whole? Three literary forms present themselves as plausible candidates for the role: the manifesto, the modern epic, and the work of world literature. Each throws some light on the distinctive character of the text; none alone is sufficient, since the *Manifesto* ultimately transcends genre. It is a robust but problematic individuality that makes it so enduring a work.

Marx took the idea of world literature from Goethe, for whom it was the evolutionary outcome of a synthesis of national literatures. Marx grounded this idea of world literature sociologically, in the world market: 'The intellectual creations of individual nations become common property. National one-sidedness and narrow-mindedness become more and more impossible, and from the numerous national and local literatures there arises a world literature.' Clearly, for Marx himself, the *Communist Manifesto* aspired to be such a work of world literature, on a par in its formal literary appeal to the breadth of the political appeal of the slogan on its cover, 'Workers of all countries unite!' And if dissemination in translation is anything to go by (35 languages and 544 separate editions prior to 1918, and innumerably more since),[24] it certainly succeeded more than any other work. However, as a formal, rather than a sociological concept, world literature is a problematic idea. As literary theorist Franco Moretti has pointed out, in the nineteenth century at least, rather than a world literature, there actually arose 'a planetary reproduction of a couple of national literatures that [found] themselves in a peculiarly lucky position'.[25] (He was writing about the way in which French and English novels became models to be imitated virtually everywhere.) Carried away with his theme, Marx appears to have forgotten his own account of the tendency within all markets to monopoly; at least, he was overly optimistic about the de-nationalization of literary markets. Rather than being the new form to which both Goethe and Marx aspired, what there has been of world literature to date has actually been more of a series of hegemonic regional literatures, within which just a few texts stand out as in some way more fundamentally 'worldly' than others.

These texts have been referred to as modern epics. The modern epic is that rare beast in which the idea of a 'world text' finds something close to an approximation. (Moretti, for example, picks out Goethe's *Faust* and Joyce's *Ulysses* in particular.) Modern epics are encyclopaedic texts that totalize at two levels: the supranational dimension of the space they represent (figuring that of the world market, albeit often allegorically); and literary styles and conventions, which they appropriate omnivorously.[26] The *Communist Manifesto* certainly fits this model. But it is not, strictly speaking, a fictional text. In this respect, the *Manifesto* is *more* than a modern epic, or at least, more than other modern epics – a kind of über-modern epic, perhaps. This 'more' is related to its overarching, synthesizing use of the manifesto form. The manifesto is a form that compels an extraordinary compression of content into a short text. The *Manifesto*'s 'more' is at the same time less. Walter Benjamin summed up the practical logic of such literary compression in the opening fragment of 'One-Way Street' (1928). Under the conditions of capitalist modernity, he argued:

> Significant literary effectiveness can come into being only in a strict alternation between action and writing; it must nurture the inconspicuous forms that fit its influence in active communities better than does the pretentious, universal gesture of the book – in leaflets, brochures, articles, and placards.[27]

And, one might add, manifestos. This is the closest thing to a reading of the *Manifesto* left to us by Benjamin, the twentieth century's foremost philosopher of images.

Unlike the other compositional elements of the text, Marx

did not find the manifesto form ready-made – although there were a few examples of this use of the term of which he would have been aware.[28] Most of the characteristics we now take to be distinctive of a manifesto – used particularly by the early-twentieth-century avant-gardes of Dada, Futurism and Surrealism – were defined by the *Communist Manifesto* itself. A manifesto is primarily a performance, which uses language to enact a will to realize a particular future. It aims to orientate the reader towards a specific future. This wilfulness manifests itself in a special kind of literary absolutism – the use of the tense of the absolute present – in which what is desired is presented *as if* it were already the case, in order that it might become so. In the words of the Dadaist Tristan Tzara, a manifesto must 'organize prose into a form that is absolutely and irrefutably obvious'.[29] Herein lies the manifesto's affinity to, yet difference from, fiction. This is the sense in which a manifesto always involves a pre-emption, a gamble on the future: it is written as if its vision of the future is assured, precisely because it is not. Marxism has been long plagued by its critics over Marx's claim that communism is inevitable. But this is to misunderstand Marx's use of language as action, treating it as a scientific prediction. Hence the subsequent need for the slogan 'Socialism or Barbarism!' to clarify the character of the claim.

The *Communist Manifesto* is distinctive in investing its various performative aspects ('Workers of all countries unite!') with the authority of a historical narrative about class struggle ('The history of all hitherto existing society is the history of class struggle'), which claims theoretical justification. It makes a new kind of intellectual-political claim. It is this mixture of exhortation with theoretically grounded world-history that makes it so peculiar an epic – in manifesto form. The narrative is a complicated one because it involves several different kinds of subject: pre-eminently, class subjects (the bourgeoisie, the proletariat), but also systemic subjects (free trade, capital) and, ultimately, human productive forces themselves. The articulation of these different narratives is the work of the literary form of the text, rather than of more strictly theoretical considerations. This leaves the reader suspended between theory and allegory: classes appear as allegorical subjects of systemic contradictions. The bourgeoisie acts because it is compelled to do so: 'It *must* nestle everything, settle everywhere, establish connections everywhere'; it '*cannot exist without* constantly revolutionizing the instruments of production'. And it is compelled to act so by competition: the system of free trade, which is itself the result of private property in the means of production. (Hence Marx's famous revolutionary defence of free trade in his lecture on the topic in January 1847: free trade 'hastens the social revolution', *MECW* 6, 465.) The revolutionary role of the bourgeoisie is dictated by the script of a system. Yet the bourgeoisie is nonetheless the subject of this drama; it is nonetheless a revolutionary agent of history for all that. Allegory closes the gap between condition and act.

Today, the *Manifesto*'s conflation of the bourgeoisie with capital (at one point, Marx wrote 'the bourgeoisie, *i.e.*, capital', *MECW* 6, 490) is profoundly problematic. Viewed as a historical agent, the bourgeoisie is a nationally politically organized social class, while capital is an impersonal, transnational, ideally objective social form that dominates and places structural constraints upon social classes, with which the bourgeoisie cannot be considered simply identical. At the time of the *Manifesto*, Marx had yet to develop his innovative account of capital as a form of value: 'self-expanding value'. This only happens in those parts of *Capital* written in the early 1860s. The *Manifesto*'s allegorical conflation of the political role of the bourgeoisie with capital covers over the gap between political and economic forms, out of which the possibilities of history flow. On the other hand, with regard to the proletariat, Marx made the reverse error: he treated the proletariat as a social class that exists politically almost wholly outside of capital. Yet, as the development of capitalism has illustrated, again and again, the importance of labour to capital (which Marx later acknowledged in the concept of labour as 'variable capital') infuses the *political* existence of the working class in a variety of ways that undermine its projected role as representative of a new, communistic mode of production. Marx recognized one of these when he wrote: 'This organization of the proletarians into a class, and consequently into a political party, is continually being upset again by the competition between the workers themselves.' However, he continued in the manifesto-mode of the absolute present: 'But it ever rises up again, stronger, firmer, mightier' (*MECW* 6, 493). Will and exhortation override uncertainty, presenting a kind of inevitability. This is what manifestos do. But their claim for inevitability marks a desire, not a fact: a desire for change.

It is this quasi-fictional, desiring character of the *Manifesto* that allows its first section to live on as a political text, beyond the immediate circumstances of its composition, as an image of capitalism, the fundamental social structure and dynamics of which, at a global level, remain unchanged. We can see this in capital's current 'revolutionary' transformation of China.

8

THE PLEA OF THE WORKER

The capitalist has bought the labour-power at its daily value. The use value of the labour-power belongs to him throughout one working day. He has thus acquired the right to make the worker work for him during one day. But what is a working day? At all events, it is less than a natural day. How much less? The capitalist has his own view of this point of no return, the necessary limit of the working day. As a capitalist he is only capital personified. His soul is the soul of capital. But capital has one single life-force, the drive to valorize itself, to create surplus-value, to make its constant part, the means of production, absorb the greatest possible amount of surplus labour. Capital is dead labour which, vampire-like, lives only by sucking living labour, and lives the more, the more labour it sucks. The time during which the worker works is the time during which the capitalist consumes the labour-power he has bought from him. If the worker consumes his disposable time for himself, he robs the capitalist.

The capitalist therefore takes his stand on the law of commodity-exchange. Like all other buyers, he seeks to extract the maximum possible benefit from the use-value of his commodity. Suddenly, however, there arises the voice of the worker, which had previously been stifled in the sound and fury of the production process:

'The commodity I have sold you differs from the ordinary crowd of commodities in that its use creates value, a greater value than it costs. That is why you bought it. What appears on your side as the valorization of capital is on my side an excess expenditure of labour-power. You and I know in the marketplace only one law, that of the exchange of commodities. And the consumption of the commodity belongs not to the seller who parts with it, but to the buyer who acquires it. The use of my daily labour-power therefore belongs to you. But by means of the price you pay for it every day, I must be able to reproduce it every day, thus allowing myself to sell it again. Apart from natural deterioration through age etc, I must be able to work tomorrow with the same normal amount of strength, health and freshness as today. You are constantly preaching to me the gospel of "saving" and "abstinence". Very well! Like a sensible, thrifty owner of property I will husband my sole wealth, my labour-power, and abstain from wasting it foolishly. Every day I will spend, set in motion, transfer into labour only as much of it as is compatible with its normal duration and healthy development. By an unlimited extension of the working day, you may in one day use up a quantity of labour-power greater than I can restore in three. What you gain in labour I lose in the substance of labour. Using my labour and despoiling it are quite different things . . . You may be a model citizen, perhaps a member of the RSPCA, and you may be in the odour of sanctity as well; but the thing you represent when you come face to face with me has no heart in its breast. What seems to throb there is my own heartbeat. I demand a normal working day because, like every other seller, I demand the value of my commodity.'

. . . There is here therefore an antinomy, of right against right, both equally bearing the seal of the law of exchange. Between equal rights, force decides. Hence, in the history of capitalist production, the establishment of a norm for the working day presents itself as a struggle over the limits of that day, a struggle between collective capital, i.e. the class of capitalists, and collective labour, i.e. the working class.

Extract from 'The Limits of the Working Day',
Capital: A Critique of Political Economy, Volume 1, 1867

The *Communist Manifesto* presents the bourgeoisie as the subject – the 'principle of activity' – of capitalism and the proletariat as the subject of communism. In *Capital*, on the other hand, two decades later, Marx methodologically reduced the bourgeois, the capitalist, to 'capital personified' and the proletariat to labour. It is as if he had retrospectively acknowledged the allegorical character of the *Manifesto*'s narrative. As he explained in the preface to the first edition of *Capital, Volume 1* (1867):

individuals are dealt with here only in so far as they are the personifications of economic categories, the bearers [*Träger*] of particular class-relations and interests. My standpoint, from which the economic formation of society is viewed as a process of natural history, can less than any other make the individual responsible for relations whose creature she remains, socially speaking, however much she may subjectively raise herself above them. (*C* 1, 92)

Far from the bourgeois class being the source of historical action, it is now viewed as no more than the human 'support' of processes that display the logic of a system. The subject – the 'principle of activity' – of this system is capital itself. Capital is understood by Marx in *Capital* as a particular form of value: 'self-expanding' value, grounded in the commodity, which is the elementary form of value. As such, it is not a merely physical thing – means of production – but is itself a social relation: social relations 'constitute' wealth as capital. Capital expands by entering into relations with other commodities. In production, the value of capital expands as it absorbs surplus labour – labour it extracts from the worker which is over and above the value of the worker's labour-power. Capital absorbs surplus labour by purchasing labour-power as a commodity and putting it to work as 'variable capital' – that portion of capital that has the ability to create value. Capital thus appears to have a 'life-force' of its own: 'the drive to valorize itself, to create surplus-value, to make its constant part, the means of production, absorb the greatest possible amount of surplus labour'.

The extract for this chapter explores some of the political consequences of capital as a form of value by focusing on the different relationships that capitalists and workers have to 'life' and to time. It is a wonderful example of the way in which, in *Capital*, Marx considered economic relations in their broadest, existential and political significance. The extract combines a complex theoretical argument with a polemical, confrontational use of direct speech. We can see once again a gothic imaginary in Marx's depiction of capitalism and the use of montage to incorporate historical material directly into the body of his texts. As he acknowledged in a footnote, the plea of the worker, rendered in direct speech, draws upon the manifesto of the strike committee of London building workers, issued during their strike in 1859–60 for a reduction of the working day to nine hours. (The description of the capitalist as being 'in the odour of sanctity', for example, originally referred to a certain Sir M. Peto, who was considered 'greatest profit-monger among the building masters'. He subsequently went bankrupt, Marx tells us, with a certain relish.)

The main difference between Marx's early and later critiques of political economy was his discovery of the capacity of human labour-power to produce more than its own value. Whereas in the *1844 Manuscripts*, Marx focused on labour as a process of 'objectification' (which private property converted into estrangement), in *Capital* labour is primarily viewed as a process of creating value. Labour-power is the *only* commodity that can create 'a greater value than it costs'. Here is the key to Marx's critique of political economy in *Capital*. Engels described it as 'the special law of motion governing the present-day capitalist mode of production and the bourgeois society that this mode of production has created' ('Speech at the Graveside of Karl Marx', *MECW* 24, 464).

Marx's account of the creation of surplus value depends upon a distinction between labour as an activity and labour-power as a capacity, which was missing from his earlier writings. It is labour-power, not labour, Marx argued in *Capital*, which is purchased for wages. Surplus is generated out of the difference between the value of the labour-power and the value produced during the activity of labour. It is because the capitalist appropriates this surplus that Marx described workers as 'exploited'. They do not receive the surplus they produce. This is the technical meaning of 'exploitation' within Marx's critique of political economy. The various miseries of the labour process itself are the result of the capitalist's need to generate this surplus, to 'extract' a surplus from the worker, over and above the value of his or her labour-power. In this respect, for Marx, *all* capitalists 'exploit' their workers, so long as they make a profit, not just the ones who might be considered to treat them especially badly; and the greater the profit they make, the more they exploit their workers. This is as true of so-called 'ethical capitalism' as it is of any other type of capital.

Marx, in two ways, draws on a gothic discourse of the living and the dead in his account of the working day. On the one hand, capital is described as 'dead labour' because the part of it that remains constant in value (does not 'expand') – buildings, machinery, components – is the product of previous labours, 'objectified activity', in the sense of the *1844 Manuscripts*. The labour here is dead in the sense that it is static, without a principle of movement; a mere result, spent. Capital as dead labour is contrasted to the 'living labour' of workers. On the other hand, capital exhibits a form of *living* death because it 'sucks' or 'consumes' living labour, and it 'lives the more, the more labour it sucks'. Capital 'consumes' living labour because capitalist production uses up the commodity of labour-power in the labour process. After a certain period of time, workers need rest and replenishment: their power to work has been temporarily exhausted, consumed. This consumption brings the dead labour of 'constant' capital to life by using it as a part of a process of the production of value: specifically, a surplus of value over and above the value of the capital deployed in production, including the value of the labour-power consumed. Put to work, living labour (variable capital) *revives* dead labour (constant capital), giving it movement, allowing it to transfer part of its value to the product.

Capital is vampiric because its 'single life-force – the drive to valorize itself, to create new surplus value' – can only find expression in a parasitic relation to living labour, which it incorporates into itself as variable capital. Capital exhibits movement – 'lives' – in the sense that it 'expands', grows quantitatively, as a result of relations internal to itself: the relation between variable and constant capital, labour and other means of production. It can do this only as a result of its literal consumption of the working time (and hence portion of the lives) of workers, a transformation of their time into value. This is how capital self-expands. It is something of a cross between a vampire and a zombie, feeding off living labour in order to maintain itself as a form of the living dead. Marx was mixing his metaphors once again.

Moreover, capital will try to extract as much value-creating labour as possible from the worker. In Marx's account, there are two ways of doing this. Either capital can try to make the worker work longer for a fixed wage (a 'day' rate, for example, as was common in the nineteenth century); or it can increase the productivity of labour in various ways, producing more value within a given period of time (by introducing new machinery, for example). Marx called the first, the production of 'absolute' surplus-value, and the second, 'relative' surplus-value. The length of the working day places a limit on the production of absolute surplus-value. In order to produce more value, beyond this limit, capital has to switch its strategy of exploitation and extract relative surplus-value, which involves changes in the character of the production process. New technologies become productive at the point at which they become cheaper to produce than the labour-power they displace.

However, the consumption of the worker's time in production is also the consumption of his or her life. Time has an existential as well as an economic significance. We exist in time, and it is time that gives meaning to our existence, because our time is limited: we will die. Indeed, time has an economic significance precisely because it has an existential significance. Would time be a measure of value if we were immortal? There is an existential as well as an economic significance to the distribution of activities in time. Capital's attempt 'to extract the maximum possible benefit from the use-value of [its] commodity' is consequently met with resistance from the worker whose time (and hence life) this involves. A struggle ensues over the limits of the working day. Nowadays, this is often euphemistically called 'work-life balance'. This struggle is part of a politics of time.

The words Marx put in the mouth of the worker present capital's consumption of labour-power from the worker's viewpoint, as the consumption of his or her life. Everything hinges on the value of labour-power itself. In Marx's account, the value of a commodity is determined by the 'socially average' time needed to produce it (including the labour-time embedded in its components and means of production). So the value of labour-power will be determined by the 'socially average' time of its production: the production of the worker himself or herself in a condition fit to work. In the case of skilled labour, this includes the time of education and training. But Marx always started out by examining social relations in their most basic forms and he was dealing here with the simplest case of manual labour.

For the worker, the length of the working day is an existential issue: the worker needs to reproduce his or her existence, not merely in value terms, but actually, physiologically and psychologically. Health and safety at work is no longer just about physical danger and exhaustion. It is more about stress, 'burn-out' and the mind-numbing repetitiveness of certain tasks. But the same principles apply. This existential dimension carries with it a personal imperative, which also has a moral force: 'I *must* be able to reproduce [my labour-power] every day, thus allowing myself to sell it again'; 'I *must* be able to work tomorrow with the same normal amount of strength, health and freshness as today.' Otherwise I will be unable to subsist. My existence will be imperilled. The problem for the worker is that the labour process itself may be so arduous as to consume more of the worker himself or herself – more of the worker's 'life' – than can be restored in the intervening period, despite the fact that labour-power has been purchased at its value.

Rather than merely consuming labour-power, capital would then be 'despoiling' the worker, even though it has obeyed the law of exchange. But capital is indifferent to this. It 'has no heart in its breast'. And in so far as the capitalist is capital personified, neither does the capitalist. All that capital cares about is that the law of exchange has been obeyed, and that more labour is available. It has no concern for the reproduction of the lives of individual workers. Capital has various ways of replenishing the supply of labour should the existing workforce get 'used up': drawing upon the 'reserve army' of the unemployed, immigration, or moving its production to a location which better suits its drive to create value (as is currently occurring in the on-going relocation to East Asia of a significant proportion of European manufacturing industry). The worker's 'right' to a labour process that does not consume more of the worker himself or herself than can be restored goes unrecognized by capital.

What we have here are two different conceptions of human reproduction: one, held by capital, based solely on the value of labour-power; the other, held by the worker, based on the actual demands of production and reproduction – what is 'taken out' of the worker as a finite being by capital's maximization of a surplus. This is a classic example of the way capitalism as an economic system ignores the finitude of human beings. In this respect, capital is a genuinely inhuman force. When the right of the worker (to reproduce his or her life) faces the right of the capitalist (to extract a surplus, so long as labour-power has been bought at its value), we have a confrontation between two quite different interpretations of the same law of exchange.

Workers' demands lead to a struggle because the peculiarity of labour-power as a commodity makes the capitalist system of exchange internally contradictory. There is 'an antinomy of right against right': the right of the worker and the right of the capitalist. (An antinomy is a contradiction between two equally demonstrable propositions or laws.) And between equal rights, 'force decides'. Marx used the word *Gewalt* here, which has connotations of violence. It is struggles such as these that determine the trajectory of capitalist development. For if collective labour achieves its goal of a 'normal' working day (itself historically variable, as is 'the human' itself), capital will have to switch its attention to increasing productivity, where the struggle will begin anew on a fresh footing. In general, however, it is striking how little less we work today than workers did at the end of the nineteenth century.

9

'SO-CALLED ORIGINAL ACCUMULATION'

. . . the accumulation of capital presupposes surplus-value; surplus-value presupposes capitalist production; capitalist production presupposes the availability of considerable masses of capital and labour-power in the hands of commodity producers. The whole movement, therefore seems to turn around in a never-ending circle, which we can only get out of by assuming a primitive [*ursprüngliche*, 'original'] accumulation (the 'previous accumulation' of Adam Smith) which precedes capitalist accumulation; an accumulation which is not the result of the capitalist mode of production but its point of departure.

This primitive [original] accumulation plays approximately the same role in political economy as original sin does in theology. Adam bit the apple and thereupon sin fell on the human race. Its origin is supposed to be explained when it is told as an anecdote about the past. In times long gone there were two sorts of people; one, the diligent, intelligent and above all frugal elite; the other, lazy rascals, spending their substance, and more, in riotous living. The legend of the theological original sin certainly tells us how humankind came to be condemned to eat his bread in the sweat of his brow; but the history of the economic original sin reveals to us that there are people to whom this is by no means essential. Never mind! Thus it came to pass that the former accumulated wealth and the latter finally had nothing to sell but their own skins. Since then has existed the poverty of the great mass of people who, despite their labour, have nothing to sell but themselves, and the wealth of the few, which increases constantly, although they have long ceased to work. Such insipid childishness is every day preached to us in the defence of property . . . But as soon as the question of property is at stake, it becomes a sacred duty to proclaim the standpoint of the nursery tale as the one thing fit for all age-groups and all stages of development. In actual history, it is a notorious fact that conquest, enslavement, robbery, murder, in short, violence, play the greatest part. In the tender annals of political economy the idyll always reigns. Right and 'labour' were always the sole means of enrichment, 'this year' of course always excepted. As a matter of fact, the methods of primitive [original] accumulation are anything but idyllic.

In themselves, money and commodities are no more capital than the means of production and subsistence are. They need to be transformed into capital. But this transformation can itself only take place under particular circumstances, which meet together at this point: the confrontation of, and the contact between two very different kinds of commodity owners: on the one hand, the owners of money, means of production, means of subsistence, who are eager to valorize the sum of values they have appropriated by buying the labour-power of others; on the other hand, free workers, sellers of their own labour-power, and therefore sellers of labour. Free workers, in the double sense that they neither form part of the means of production themselves, as would be the case with slaves, serfs, etc, nor do they own the means of production, as would be the case with self-employed peasant proprietors. They are therefore free from, unencumbered by, any means of production of their own. With this splitting of the commodity-market the fundamental conditions of capitalist production are given. The capital-relation presupposes a complete separation between workers and the ownership of the conditions for the realization of their labour. As soon as capitalist production stands on its own feet, it not only maintains this separation, but reproduces it on a constantly extending scale. The process that creates the capital-relation can be nothing other than the process that divorces the worker from the ownership of the conditions of his or her own labour. This is a process that on the one hand, transforms the social means of subsistence and production into capital, and on the other hand, transforms the immediate producers into wage-labourers. So-called primitive [original] accumulation, therefore, is nothing but the historical process of divorcing the producer from the means of production. It appears as 'primitive' [original] because it forms the pre-history of capital, and of the mode of production corresponding to capital. . . .

In the history of primitive [original] accumulation, all revolutions are epoch-making that act as levers for the capitalist class in its formation; but, above all, those moments when great human masses are suddenly and forcibly torn from their means of subsistence, and hurled onto the labour-market, rightless and unprotected, as free proletarians. The expropriation of the agricultural producer, of the peasant, from the soil is the basis of the whole process. The history of

this expropriation assumes different aspects in different
countries, and runs through its various phases in different
orders of succession, and in different historical epochs.

Extract from 'The Secret of Original Accumulation',
Capital: A Critique of Political Economy, Volume 1, 1867

The first volume of Marx's *Capital* expounds the fundamental elements and dynamics of capital – the commodity, money,
capital itself as a form of value, labour, surplus-value and accumulation – with only occasional historical digressions. It
presupposes the existence of capitalism and sets out to explain
to the reader precisely what it is and how it functions.
However, the volume ends with a self-contained discussion of
the historical conditions that lead to capitalist production,
'So-called Original Accumulation'.[30] These chapters are best
known for the account they give of the transition to capitalism in England from the fifteenth to the eighteenth centuries,
where, Marx argued, the pre-history of capitalism appears in
'classic form'. They have tended to be read as 'merely' historical, in the sense of being solely about the past. However, as
Marx made clear, he was concerned with the social conditions
for capitalist production in general. England is simply the
exemplar. As more and more societies become subject to the
economic forms of capitalism today – the ex-socialist states of
Eastern Europe and China, in particular – this final part of the
first volume of *Capital* becomes of especial contemporary
political relevance. It is about expropriation, illegality and
violence.

Aveling's 1888 rendering of the German *ursprüngliche Akku-
mulation* as 'primitive accumulation' (surprisingly retained in
Fowkes's 1976 translation) is particularly inappropriate in this
context. It belongs to a nineteenth-century anthropological
imagery, which would consign the process to a past time; or at

least, identifies its methods as those of pre-history. Yet they are at the forefront of current transformations in global capitalism. I have translated the phrase more literally as 'original accumulation'. The concept of origin, *Ursprung*, has an important place in German philosophy, especially in the twentieth century. (It is central to the thought of both Martin Heidegger and Walter Benjamin, for example.) Its literal meaning, 'source' – etymologically, *Ur-Sprung*, first leap or jump – should be kept in mind, since it implies a constantly renewed production. Original accumulation is original in this precise sense: it lies at the basis of capital accumulation wherever and whenever such a process begins.

In this extract, Marx was concerned to do two things: to dispel the myth perpetrated by political economy about the origins of capitalism in personal abstinence and the consequently moral character of its basic inequality; and to replace this myth with his own account of the actual historical origins of capitalism in violent and illegal processes of expropriation. Along the way, he provided a useful clarification of what he meant by capitalism as a mode of production, which is something quite different from the increasingly popular notion of a market society, with which capitalism is now frequently confused. Marx classified societies according to the way they produce surpluses; the neo-classical economic notion of a market society classifies them according to the extent of exchange relations within them. However, as Marx pointed out, the world market developed from the end of the fifteenth century onwards, within feudalism, along with merchant capital and the growth of cities as centres of trading. This was nearly 200 years before capitalism established itself as a mode of production in England. These trading relations – made possible by the appropriation of surplus through tax and feudal rent – sustained the consumption habits of the feudal nobility (inherited from the ruling classes of the Roman empire) for whom luxury imported items such silks and spices functioned politically as both display and reward.[31]

The myth of capitalism's origin presented in political economy derives from an argument about the 'state of nature' that the seventeenth-century English philosopher John Locke set out in the second of his *Two Treatises of Government* (1690). Locke imagined a state of nature prior to civil society in which men are free and equal but nonetheless governed by a 'natural law', ordained by God, which gives them the right to life and liberty, so long as they do not infringe the 'natural rights' of others. These natural rights involve property in one's own body and, by extension, in the product of one's own labour. All social laws must be justified by being derived, via legitimate contracts, from this situation. Political economy justifies the unequal social distribution of wealth, which capitalism inherits, as the result of a difference in the moral qualities of individuals in this situation. In Marx's words, there are 'two sorts of people; one, the diligent, intelligent and above all frugal elite; the other lazy rascals, spending their substance, and more, in riotous living'. The diligent and frugal accumulate, the lazy rascals squander, until the latter have to look to the former for employment in order to subsist.

Marx ridiculed the 'insipid childishness' of this Lockean 'nursery tale', told by Adam Smith in *The Wealth of Nations* (1776), as equivalent in its structure and credibility to the biblical explanation of the origin of sin. Although, as Marx pointed out, the economic version exempts an entire social class from the consequences of original sin (being condemned to eat one's bread in the sweat of one's brow), since the diligence and frugality of their forbearers' 'original accumulation' has exempted them from labour. Marx implied that this moral

justification of the class inequality upon which capitalism
depends is in fact, within its own Christian terms, irreligious.

But this is just a passing dig at the religious hypocrisy of the
bourgeoisie. Marx's main point is methodological. It concerns the anachronistic application to pre-capitalist situations
of concepts that are historically specific to capitalism. This is
flagrant in Locke's description of the state of nature, where he
attributed the capitalistic concept of private property to a pre-
social condition. It applies equally to any account of 'original'
accumulation that presupposes that a prior accumulation of
wealth alone is sufficient in itself to establish capitalist production. All such accounts naturalize the class relations upon
which capitalism depends by assuming that they already exist
prior to capitalism. Political economy assumes that a prior
accumulation of wealth is the only historical condition of
capitalism.[32]

For Marx, on the other hand, the main question was not
'How did an accumulation of wealth come about prior to
capitalism, which was subsequently invested in capitalist production?', but 'How did the social relations of capitalist
production become established, such that previously accumulated wealth could take the social form of capital?' For
Marx, capitalism is defined by the social relations of production, the capital-labour relation – not by exchange (markets),
a particular level of accumulation, or any particular techniques
of production. 'In themselves, money and commodities are no
more capital than the means of production and subsistence are.
They need to be transformed into capital.' To be transformed
into capital, wealth has to be used to create value. This
depends upon the commodification of labour-power, the
source of value.

According to Marx, there is not one, but two fundamental
conditions for capitalist production:

> on the one hand, the owners of money, means of produc-
> tion, means of subsistence, who are eager to valorize the
> sum of values they have appropriated by buying the labour-
> power of others; on the other hand, free workers, sellers of
> their own labour-power, and therefore sellers of labour.

Moreover, it is the second of these conditions that is more
important, not the first. For the process by which the class of
wage-workers is formed – 'a complete separation between
workers and the ownership of the conditions for the realization of their labour' – is the very same process by which land
is freed from the complex constraints of the feudal rights of
tenants, to become available for use as capital. In the paradigm-
atic case, where capitalism develops out of feudalism in
England, free feudal peasant proprietors, with tenants rights
over the land, were 'suddenly and forcibly torn from their
means of subsistence, and hurled onto the labour-market,
rightless and unprotected [relative to their previous feudal
rights], as free proletarians.' (Marx pointed out that in
England, 'serfdom had disappeared in practice by the last part
of the fourteenth century.' *C* 1, 877) The expropriation of the
peasantry freed the land to be appropriated as private – that is,
capitalistic – property, by the lords, as the basis of a capitalist
agriculture.

Marx provided a detailed summary of this process, as it
occurred in England from the last third of the fifteenth century
until the middle of the nineteenth century – a period of transition of nearly 400 years. Commentators have tended to
emphasize Marx's account of the enclosures of the common
land, but this is only one of four main forms of expropriation
in England that he discussed. The others are the 'colossal spo-
liation' of the property of the Catholic Church during the
sixteenth-century Reformation, the 'fraudulent alienation of

state domains' after the so-called Glorious Revolution of 1688, and 'the usurpation of feudal and clan property and its transformation into modern private property under circumstances of ruthless terrorism' in the so-called 'clearing of estates' in the eighteenth and early nineteenth centuries (C 1, 877–95). All play a role in laying the foundation for a transformation of feudal property into private property that has as its condition the dispossession of the peasantry from the land. Original accumulation, far from being the product of diligence and abstinence, is actually expropriation. As such, it was both illegal (at the time) and necessarily violent.

Furthermore, Marx argued, this violence was not restricted to the act of dispossession, which created an army of beggars and vagabonds. Violence was also required to transform the dispossessed peasantry from vagabonds and beggars into wage-labourers (a condition that they were by no means initially inclined to embrace). However, this second violence was the legal violence of an anachronistic law that criminalized the newly 'free' peasant and proto-worker who was without employment, on the basis of the presumption of the old, feudal conditions of existence: namely, that he had access to means of subsistence. The newly freed peasant was thus forced to become a wage-labourer.

The length and historical complexity of this process is important. For whereas political revolutions are generally measured in months – at most, a few years – social revolutions, which mark the transition from one mode of production to another, are measured in centuries. They are extraordinarily complex historical events and, not surprisingly, Marx's emphasis on the dispossession of the peasantry as the single main factor driving this process has been contested. In particular, it has been suggested that commerce in cities played a crucial independent role in promoting capitalist development.[33]

However, Marx acknowledged the expansion of wool manufacture in Flanders (and a rise in the price of wool) as providing the 'direct impulse' for the evictions that made the first enclosures possible, since it motivated those he called 'the new nobility' to convert arable land into pasture for sheep. To do this, they had to evict the peasantry then working the land. Marx's point, though, is that this commercial impulse was not in itself sufficient to establish the conditions for *capitalist* production, since, for Marx, capitalism requires not merely production for a market (which predates capitalism), but production based on wage-labour. Only then does the law of value come into effect. The law of value regulates competition between producers and drives accumulation; only under these conditions can capital accumulation become systemic. Marx is prepared to acknowledge as part of original accumulation anything that can be shown to 'act as a lever for the capitalist class in its formation'. But there is no capitalism without wage-labour, since in Marx's conception capital is not 'stock', but a certain *social relation*.

Marx called this process 'so-called' original accumulation for two reasons. First, as we have seen, because it is actually an expropriation; whereas the term accumulation tends to lend the process a certain legitimacy. Second, and more fundamentally, because it is not a single, one-off act, but an *on-going* historical process. It occurs wherever there is a transition to capitalism, but also *within* certain kinds of capitalist societies themselves, where the capital-labour relation is dominant, but significant amounts of non-capitalistic economic activity remain, which function as a resource for renewed bouts of 'original accumulation'. In this regard, one might say, capitalism has a perpetual need for something like original accumulation, in order to renew itself internally by extending the separation between labour and the conditions for its realization to more and more spheres of human activity. This is precisely what has been occurring, in a piecemeal fashion, in India and Latin America for the last two centuries. However, the most significant current bout of original accumulation has been happening within the ex-Soviet Socialist Republics and the People's Republic of China, over the last fifteen years. Societies that had considered themselves 'post-capitalist' have once again become centres for capital accumulation, and they have had to undergo 'original' accumulation all over again.[34]

The transition from state socialism to capitalism is certainly different from the transition from feudalism to capitalism; and it is different in different state socialist societies. In Russia, for example, the starting point is not primarily agricultural but a type of state ownership of industrial production. But the same basic principles of expropriation, illegality and violence apply to the rigged auctions privatizing state assets in Russia in the 1990s as they did to 'the fraudulent alienation of the state domains' in England at the end of the seventeenth century. From Marx's point of view, it could not be any other way. Marx was a historical realist who acknowledged the amorality and violence of history, and condemned the hypocrisy of those who would present such events in essentially moral terms. For Marx, the historical meaning of such events was ultimately to be judged according to the possibilities for humanity opened up by the social developments in question, not within the lifetime of those affected by them, but in the long term. As we shall see in the next chapter, in the context of capitalist colonialism, this kind of speculative historical realism has been highly contentious.

10

COLONIALISM: THE 'HIDEOUS PAGAN IDOL' OF PROGRESS

India . . . could not escape the fate of being conquered, and the whole of her past history, if it be anything, is the history of the successive conquests she has undergone. Indian society has no history at all, at least no known history. What we call its history is but the history of the successive intruders who founded their empires on the passive basis of that unresisting and unchanging society. The question, therefore, is not whether the English had a right to conquer India, but whether we are to prefer India conquered by the Turk, by the Persian, by the Russian, to India conquered by the Briton.

England has to fulfil a double mission in India; one destructive, the other regenerating – the annihilation of old Asiatic society, and the laying of the material foundations of western society in Asia. . . .

[The British] destroyed [Hindu civilization] by breaking up the native communities, by uprooting the native industry, and by levelling all that was great and elevated in the native society. The historical pages of their rule in India report hardly anything beyond that destruction. The work of regeneration hardly transpires through a heap of ruins. Nevertheless it has begun. . . .

Modern industry, resulting from the railway system, will dissolve the hereditary divisions of labour, upon which rest the Indian castes, those decisive impediments to Indian progress and Indian power.

All the English bourgeoisie will be forced to do will neither emancipate nor materially mend the social condition of the mass of the people, which is dependent not only on the development of the productive powers, but on their appropriation by the people. But what they will not fail to do is to lay down the material premises for both. Has the bourgeoisie ever done more? Has it ever effected a progress without dragging individuals and peoples through blood and dirt, through misery and degradation? . . .

The devastating effects of English industry, when contemplated with regard to India, a country as vast as Europe, and containing 150 million acres, are palpable and confounding. But we must not forget that they are only the organic results of the whole system of production as it is now constituted. That production rests on the supreme rule of capital. The centralization of capital is essential to the existence of capital as an independent power. The destructive influence of that centralization upon the markets of the world does but reveal, in the most gigantic dimensions, the inherent organic laws of political economy now at work in every civilized town. The bourgeois period of history has to create the material basis of the new world – on the one hand the universal intercourse founded upon the mutual dependency of mankind, and the means of that intercourse; on the other hand the development of the productive powers of humankind and the transformation of material production into a scientific domination of natural

agencies. Bourgeois industry and commerce create these
material conditions of a new world in the same way as geo-
logical revolutions have created the surface of the earth.
When a great social revolution shall have mastered the
results of the bourgeois epoch, the market of the world
and the modern powers of production, and subjected them
to the common control of the most advanced peoples, then
only will human progress cease to resemble that hideous
pagan idol, who would not drink the nectar but from the
skulls of the slain.

Extract from 'The Future Results of the British Rule in India',
New York Daily Tribune, 8 August 1853

Marx's writings on British rule in India have been the cause of
great controversy. They have frequently served as an exemplar
of his views on capitalist colonialism, and, increasingly since
the 1960s, they have been vigorously attacked – especially by
anti-colonial nationalists, but also by some Third World
Marxists, and, more recently, liberal multi-culturalists. These
writings raise issues about the nature of colonial and post-
colonial societies; the character and scope of Marx's model of
historical development; the Eurocentrism, Orientalism and
possibly even racism in Marx's descriptions of Indian society;
and, most difficult of all, the relationship between historical
and political judgement.

The extract above comes from one of twelve dispatches
on Indian affairs that Marx wrote for the *New York Daily
Tribune* in 1853, in a series that was followed a few years later
by a further twenty-one contributions (1857–8). Marx
wrote these pieces of journalism mainly for the money,
although his interest was stimulated by the fact that India had
become an issue in domestic politics in Britain in 1853: first,
because of the renewal of the East India Company Charter,

and second, because of wrangling over a Government of India Bill. (Marx was an assiduous reader of the Parliamentary Papers.) The writings are popular, polemical and conjectural – opinion pieces – rather than an expression of new theoretical reflection, scholarship or empirical research. Marx seems to have simply applied to India the argument of the *Communist Manifesto*, first published five years earlier – or at least, applied it to what he knew about India, which was not a great deal (he made several errors), although it was also not a great deal less that the current state of historical scholarship in England at the time. There is a world of difference between the validity of a general theoretical approach to history and that of its application to a particular society at a specific moment in time, which is contingent upon amassing and mastering the relevant body of empirical knowledge. In this respect, these writings have come to bear a theoretical and political burden for which they are not well suited. It is also important to remember that the pieces were written for a North American audience. As the Indian Marxist Aijaz Ahmad has pointed out, the USA was the one society in which a colonial experience (albeit of a different variety) was giving rise to brisk capitalist development. Marx seems to have been hoping for a future for India not unlike that under way in the USA.[35]

Nonetheless, the depiction of pre-colonial India as an 'unchanging' society, without any known history, 'passive' and 'unresisting' to successive invasions, is shocking. It reproduces the most hackneyed Orientalist stereotype. (Orientalism is a Western cultural discourse about Eastern societies, with its modern origins in late eighteenth-century Europe, which presumes the superiority of the West.)[36] The description of British colonialism as 'devastating' in its socially destructive effects, 'dragging individuals and peoples through blood and dirt, through misery and degradation', does not offset this opening image. Rather, it is the other way around: the image of passivity functions to legitimate the devastation. If it were not the British, the argument goes, it would be the Turk, the Persian or the Russian; however, the British bring not just colonial rule, but capitalism, which holds the promise of economic development and, ultimately, a communist future; so that is the best option. Furthermore, in his description of the 'great social revolution' to come, Marx wrote of the common control of economic forces by 'the most advanced peoples'. It is unclear precisely who this refers to, but it appears to imply that India will have to wait for any kind of economic self-determination until after a period of benevolent socialist colonialism.

However, while Marx's account certainly contains an Orientalist depiction of the state of pre-colonial India, it does not display an Orientalist attitude towards it. This would have involved some kind of Romantic nostalgia for a golden age of Hindustan – an attitude expressly rejected by Marx early on in his first dispatch. Marx acknowledged much that was 'great and elevated' about what he called 'Hindu civilization', but he also wrote, elsewhere in the piece from which our extract is taken: 'Nowhere more than in India do we meet with social destitution in the midst of plenty, for want of the means of exchange.' And he identified 'the hereditary divisions of labour, upon which rest the Indian castes' as the 'decisive impediments to Indian progress and Indian power'. In these respects, his tendency is to equate pre-colonial India with feudalism in Europe: a society characterized by the political domination of a hereditary system of particular interests. In the *Communist Manifesto*, feudalism is the only immediately pre-capitalist mode of production discussed. Marx took the transition from feudalism to capitalism in Europe as his model for transitions to capitalism elsewhere. In this, his perspective was not Orientalist but Eurocentric, a related but rather different cultural disposition that takes Europe as a paradigm for social development elsewhere.[37]

At this point, Marx seems to have had in mind a single model of the development of modes of production, within which capitalist colonialism, or imperialism as it became known in Marxist theory in the twentieth century, acts as a 'pioneer of capitalism' in economically less-developed, non-European societies, speeding up history.[38] Stalin subsequently turned this provisional conclusion of Marx's research in 1853 into the fixed doctrine of the 'five stages' of history – original communism–slavery–feudalism–capitalism–communism. Every society supposedly passes through each in succession. On the other hand, Marx himself, in his notebooks of the late 1850s, modified his position and proposed the concept of a distinct 'Asiatic' mode of production. This had the virtue of treating the pre-colonial history of non-European societies as an independent object of investigation. However, it reproduced the Eurocentrism of the previous view in a different form, in so far as it treats all non-European societies as subject to the *same* (non-European) economic history. The 'Asiatic' mode of production was not necessarily restricted to Asia. This led to the thesis of the 'two roads': a European road leading to capitalism and a non-European road on which economic development was blocked.

Despite these weaknesses, the recovery in the 1960s of Marx's concept of the Asiatic mode of production played an important role in moving debates beyond the intellectually arid and politically pernicious 'stagism' of the Stalinist doctrine.[39] (If societies had to become capitalist before they could become communist; and capitalism required a national bourgeoisie; then it became the ironic task of Communist Parties to further the cause of the national bourgeoisie in ex-colonial societies.) On the other hand, criticism of the overly general, problem-solving nature of Marx's notion of an 'Asiatic' mode opened up a variety of new, multilinear approaches to understanding the character of what were by then post-colonial societies. These approaches quickly moved beyond the limits of Marx's own writings. They raised fundamental questions about what Marx had meant by a 'mode of production' – was it an 'epochal' concept or could particular societies be characterized by 'mixed' modes? – and how applicable the concept was to post-colonial societies. During the 1970s, debates about colonialism, post-colonialism, underdevelopment, uneven development and dependency were the most important theoretical developments within Marxism since the debates about imperialism in the 1920s. In large part, this was because of the fruitfulness of the exchanges that occurred between Marxist and other theoretical positions ('dependency theory' and 'world systems theory', in particular) that shared with it a political interest in bettering the position of the post-colonial societies of the south within the world economy.[40]

These debates throw retrospective light on Marx's writings on India, first, by highlighting the problematic character of Marx's concept of progress, and second, by dramatizing the difficulties and dilemmas of world-historical political judgements. Marx's relationship to the notion of progress in history is a complex one. The concept is modern, dating only from the Enlightenment philosophy of history, which secularized Christian history into a linear process progressing towards the realization of human reason and freedom. At one level, Marx's work decisively rejects the linear Enlightenment view. The idea of modes of production emphasizes both historical discontinuity and social conflict, and Marx was acutely aware that history has been and continues to be (in Hegel's phrase) 'a slaughterbench'. Nonetheless, there is another level at which Marx embraces a progressivist position. For Marx, history acquires both a direction and a meaning from its economic content: the development of the forces of production, the power of productivity. This is Marx's famous 'productivism'. However, there is 'progress' here only from the perspective of a point in the future (communism) at which time the 'human' content of social productivity will become universally shared. In this respect, all claims about progress are speculative. Furthermore, although some kinds of society may be chrono-logically 'closer' to the purported end state, in themselves they are not thereby necessarily politically preferable for their mem-bers than the ones that preceded them. Given class divisions, many have no share in the opportunities for new forms of life and action made possible by the increases in productive power represented by the societies they live in. Marx's is a dialectical form of progressivism, which understands progress not in gradualist or evolutionary terms, but with reference to the ultimate resolution of a developing set of contradictions. It has an eschatological dimension: it adopts the standpoint of the 'last times'. Marx's historical view privileges the human potential of technology in the future – its potential for facili-tating new ways of being human – over wellbeing in the here and now. Indeed, Marx goes so far as to insist that prior to the 'great social revolution' progress will continue to take the form of a 'hideous pagan idol, who would not drink the nectar but from the skulls of the slain'. This is a tragic view of history, which offers little comfort to those who will be slain.[41]

For many European Marxists, the experience of fascism in Europe and the Second World War removed their hope in the social potential of capitalist technology. This led some, such as the German philosopher Theodor W. Adorno, to invert the moral content of Marx's productivism: 'No universal history leads from savagery to humanitarianism, but there is one leading from the slingshot to the megaton bomb.'[42] This is a polemical inversion worthy of Marx himself. It is noteworthy that there was no equivalent reaction from European intellectuals to the systematic violence of capitalist colonialism. However, Adorno's aphorism depends on extracting the technological aspect of Marx's idea of the forces of production from its social dimension – the productive power of social relations themselves, the new forms of collectivity represented by new divisions of labour. Under capitalism, these forms of collectivity are alienated from their human meaning. But if what it means to be human is always relative to the social relations of production, and these vary widely in different societies (even different capitalist societies) at any given time, then there is no single point of view from which to make historical judgements about the present as a whole, *except* that of a highly speculative future. Yet if the subject on whose behalf history is being made is the humanity of the future, how do the judgements made in its name relate to actual living subjects within the historical present?

This is the crucial question for Marx's world-historical conception of political judgement, which his writings on India throw into sharp relief. Marx's thought is distinctive in insisting that politics should be judged world-historically. But there are profound difficulties here. For there is a gap – in danger of widening into a gulf – between the scope of political actions and that of world-history. Political action gains its meaning from narratives that grow out of present existence, however historically extended these narratives may be. Politics has never just been about the living: people fight political battles for future generations, as much or more than for themselves; and they also do so in order to maintain, destroy or construct certain relationships with the past. But these historical per-spectives that are internal to political action are much more restricted, especially geographically, than world-history itself. Marx's 'The Future Results of British Rule in India' reminds us of this by its exclusive focus on the effects of the colonial imposition of capitalism, and its neglect of Indian history.

Marx's writings on British rule in India dramatize the prob-lematic legacy of his world-historical mode of political analysis. It is easy to dismiss them for their Eurocentric ten-dencies. Yet they lay down a challenge to their critics: to use the benefits of more extensive empirical knowledge and polit-ical hindsight to produce a more adequate account of capitalist colonialism, and its continuing effects, on the same world-historical scale. In this respect, it is the intellectual scope and theoretical ambition demanded by Marx of historical analysis that is his greatest legacy. This demand is underwritten by both his early philosophical writings and *Capital* itself. Marx's understanding of capitalism is far more historically subtle and complex than is usually thought. In insisting upon this, and upon the political significance of a genuinely global history, Marx's writings show themselves to be of far greater contem-porary relevance than those of many twentieth- and even twenty-first-century thinkers.

NOTES

1 See Sigmund Freud, 'Fetishism' (1927), in his *On Sexuality: Three Essays on the Theory of Sexuality and Other Works*, Penguin, London, 1987, pp. 351–7.

2 Max Horkheimer and Theodor W. Adorno, *Dialectic of Enlightenment: Philosophical Fragments* (1944), trans. Edmund Jephcott, Stanford University Press, Stanford, 2002.

3 G. W. F. Hegel, *Lectures on the Philosophy of World History: Introduction*, trans. H. B. Nisbet, Cambridge University Press, Cambridge, 1975, pp. 180–81.

4 See William Pietz, 'The Problem of the Fetish, 1', *Res*, 9, Spring 1985, pp. 5–17.

5 See Philippe Lacoue-Labarthe and Jean-Luc Nancy, *The Literary Absolute: The Theory of Literature in German Romanticism*, trans. Philip Barnard and Cheryl Lester, SUNY Press, New York, 1988, Ch. 1. The quotation is from Friedrich Schlegel, *Athenaeum* fragment 206.

6 The subtlety of Feuerbach's writings, and the extent to which Marx at times relied upon them at the very moment he was most fiercely criticizing them, has generally gone unrecognized. An excellent account of Feuerbach's philosophy can be found in Marx Wartofky, *Feuerbach*, Cambridge University Press, Cambridge, 1977.

7 See Friedrich Engels, *Dialectics of Nature* (1886), trans. Clement Dutt, Progress Publishers, Moscow, 1954; Joseph V. Stalin, *Dialectical and Historical Materialism* (1938), Lawrence and Wishart, London, 1940. This approach to the relationship between philosophy and science derives from late nineteenth-century neo-Kantianism with which Marx's thought has little in common.

8 Étienne Balibar, *The Philosophy of Marx*, trans. Chris Turner, Verso, London, 1995, p. 25.

9 P. N. Fedoseyev et al., *Karl Marx: A Biography*, Progress Publishers, Moscow, 1973, p. 112.

10 These two quotations come from a passage that was subsequently crossed out on the manuscript. However, since deletions of this kind on the clean copy are editorial in character, in the sense that they concern the ordering of the material, rather than changes in its intellectual content, there is no reason to suppose that Marx rejected the position they outline.

11 I explore this relation in 'One Time, One History?', in Peter Osborne, *The Politics of Time*, Verso, London and New York, 1995, Ch. 2.

12 Marx's summary of the supposed 'doctrine' of historical material-ism, in the 1859 preface to *A Contribution to a Critique of Political Economy*, is actually no more than an account of the 'general con-clusion' he had reached by 1846 from his initial study of political economy, which, he wrote, became the 'guiding principle' of his further studies. Marx pursued those studies for a further thirty-seven years after 1846, during which his methodological approach to the study of capitalism underwent a series of decisive develop-ments within this loose regulative frame.

13 'Civil society' was the term used by Adam Smith to refer to the object of political economy. In turning to political economy, Marx was thus returning to one of the original economic sources of Hegel's account of civil society.

14 See Georg Lukács, *The Young Hegel* (1948), trans. Rodney Livingstone, Merlin Press, London, 1975, p. 538; Stanley Rosen, *G. W. F. Hegel: An Introduction to the Science of Wisdom* (1974), St Augustine's Press, South Bend, 2000, pp. 173, 223, 281.

15 Immanuel Kant, *Critique of Pure Reason* (1781; 1787), trans. Paul Guyer and Allen W. Wood, Cambridge University Press, Cambridge, 1997, pp. 100–101, 643.

16 See Immanuel Kant, 'An Answer to the Question: What is Enlightenment?' (1784), in his *Perpetual Peace and Other Essays*, trans. Ted Humphreys, Hackett, Indianapolis, 1983.

17 Francis Fukuyama, *The End of History and the Last Man*, Penguin, London, 1992.

18 For an account of international communism during this period,

see Fernando Claudin, *The Communist Movement: From Comintern to Cominform*, 2 vols, Monthly Review Press, New York and London, 1975.

19 Engels produced two earlier drafts of the programme of the Communist League, 'Draft of a Communist Confession of Faith' and *Principles of Communism*, in June and October 1847, respectively. Both were in catechism form. The *Manifesto* itself was the result of a two-stage process of composition, setting out from Engels's *Principles of Communism*. Marx and Engels worked on it together in December 1847, in London and Brussels, revising and reframing Engels's earlier text. Marx then worked on it alone during January 1848, while Engels was in Paris. Marx had sole editorial responsibility for the final version.

20 Marshall Berman, *All That Is Solid Melts into Air: The Experience of Modernity*, Verso, London, 1982, p. 92.

21 See 'Modernity: A Different Time', in Osborne, *The Politics of Time*, Ch. 1.

22 Walter Benjamin, *The Arcades Project*, trans. Howard Eiland and Kevin McLaughlin, Harvard University Press, Cambridge, MA and London, 1999, p. 470, [nn. 7, 6].

23 The analysis that follows draws upon and extends the argument in 'Remember the Future? The *Communist Manifesto* as Cultural-Historical Form', in Peter Osborne, *Philosophy in Cultural Theory*, Routledge, London and New York, 2000, Ch. 4.

24 Rob Beamish, 'The Making of the Manifesto', in Leo Panitch and Colin Leys (eds.), *Socialist Register 1998. The Communist Manifesto Now*, Merlin Press, London, p. 233.

25 Franco Moretti, *Atlas of the European Novel, 1800–1900*, Verso, London and New York, 1998, p. 187.

26 See Franco Moretti, *The Modern Epic: The World-System from Goethe to García Márquez*, Verso, London and New York, 1996, pp. 1–6.

27 Walter Benjamin, 'One-Way Street', in *Selected Writings. Volume 1: 1913–1926*, ed. Marcus Bullock and Michael W. Jennings, Harvard University Press, Cambridge, MA and London, 1996, p. 444. 'Less is more' is familiar these days from a variety of uses in advertising. The slogan originates with the modernist architect Mies van de Rohe.

28 The first example is probably Sylvain Maréchals's *Manifeste des Égaux*, 1796. More immediately relevant is Victor Considèrent's *Principle of Socialism: Manifesto of the Democracy of the Nineteenth Century* (1843; 2nd edition, 1847).

29 Tristan Tzara, 'Dada Manifesto' (1918), in *Seven Dada Manifestos and Lampisteries*, trans. Barbara Wright, Calder Publications, London, 1977, p. 3.

30 This was initially a single long chapter, at the end of part 7, 'The Process of Accumulation of Capital'. However, in the English edition of 1888, Engels made it into a separate part, part 8, in order to register the difference between its subject matter and the rest of the book, and he turned the sections of the original chapter into discrete chapters.

31 See R. H. Hilton, 'Feudal Society', in Tom Bottmore, ed., *A Dictionary of Marxist Thought*, Blackwell, Oxford, 1983, pp. 166–70.

32 This Lockean argument was revived in the 1970s by the libertarian Harvard philosopher, Robert Nozick, in *Anarchy, State and Utopia*, Basic Books, New York, 1974, as a critique of the social egalitarianism of his colleague John Rawls's *A Theory of Justice* (Harvard University Press, Cambridge, MA and London, 1971). It served as an arcane philosophical justification of neo-liberalism.

33 See Rodney Hilton, ed., *The Transition from Feudalism to Capitalism*, New Left Books, London, 1976. For a more recent contribution, see Robert Brenner, *Merchants and Revolution*, Cambridge University Press, Cambridge, 1993.

34 Lenin applied Marx's concept of original accumulation to the first phase of the development of capitalism in Russia, prior to the bourgeois and socialist revolutions of the early twentieth century, in V. I. Lenin, *The Development of Capitalism in Russia* (1899), *Collected Works*, volume 3, Foreign Languages Publishing House, Moscow, 1960.

35 See Aijaz Ahmad, 'Marx on India: A Clarification', in *In Theory: Classes, Nations, Literatures*, Verso, London and New York, 1992, Ch. 6.

36 See Edward Said, *Orientalism: Western Conceptions of the Orient* (1978), Penguin, London, 1991. Said's discussion of Marx as a

case in which 'a non-Orientalist's human engagements were first dissolved, then usurped by Orientalist generalizations' (p. 156) is, however, problematic in various respects. For a critique, see Ahmad, 'Marx on India'.

37 See Samir Amin, *Eurocentrism*, trans. Russell Moore, Zed Books, London, 1989.

38 See Bill Warren, *Imperialism: Pioneer of Capitalism*, New Left Books, London, 1980.

39 See Stephen P. Dunn, *The Rise and Fall of the Asiatic Mode of Production*, Routledge, New York and London, 1982.

40 The most important texts here were André Gunder Frank, *Capitalism and Uneven Development in Latin America*, Monthly Review Press, New York, 1969; Immanuel Wallerstein, *The Modern World System*, Academic Press, New York, 1974; Samir Amin, *Unequal Development* and *Imperialism and Unequal Development* (1973), Monthly Review Press, New York, 1976 and 1977.

41 See Raymond Williams, *Modern Tragedy* (1966), Verso, London 1979, part 1.

42 Theodor W. Adorno, 'Universal History', in *Negative Dialectics* (1966), trans. E. B. Ashton, Routledge, London, 1973, p. 320.

CHRONOLOGY

1818 May 5, Marx born in Trier, Rhine Province, Prussia. Son of Heinrich, a lawyer, and Henriette (née Pressburg) from Holland. One of nine siblings.

1831 Death of Hegel.

1835 Matriculates from Gymnasium in Trier. A law student in Bonn.

1836 Studies law and philosophy in Berlin. Engagement to Jenny von Westphalen.

1838 Marx's father dies.

1839 *Notebooks on Epicurean Philosophy*.

1841 Award of doctorate *in absentia* in Jena. Feuerbach, *Essence of Christianity*.

1842 Contributes to the *Rhenish Times*; becomes editor in October.

1843 March, *Rhenish Times* closed by Prussian authorities. June, marries Jenny von Westphalen. *Kreuznach Notebooks*. Letters to Ruge. Late October, moves to Paris. 'A Contribution to the Critique of Hegel's Philosophy of Right. Introduction.'

1844 *Economic and Philosophical Manuscripts*. Birth of daughter, Jenny. Ten-day visit from Engels – beginning of their collaboration. Engels, *The Condition of the Working Class in England*.

1845 February, expelled from France, moves to Brussels. Begins *The German Ideology* (with Engels).

1846 Marx joins The League of the Just. Birth of second daughter, Laura.

1847 *Poverty of Philosophy* (a response to Proudon's *Philosophy of Poverty*). Ten-hour Bill in Britain limits the working day. Birth of son, Edgar (died, 1855). Formation of the Communist League.

1848 *Manifesto of the Communist Party*. February revolutions in Europe. Expelled from Belgium, returns to Germany. Editor of the *New Rhenish Times*. Californian gold rush.

1849 Failure of Frankfurt National Assembly. Marx acquitted of 'incitement to rebellion'. Expelled from Germany as a stateless subject. Moves to London. Birth of son, Guido (died, 1851).

1850 *Class Struggles in France.*

1851 Louis Napoléon Bonaparte's coup d'état in France.

1852 *The Eighteenth Brumaire of Louis Bonaparte.*

1853 First writings on India, *New York Daily Tribune.*

1854–6 War in Crimea.

1857–8 *Grundrisse (Foundations of the Critique of Political Economy, Rough Draft).* Baudelaire, *Les Fleurs du Mal.*

1859 *A Contribution to the Critique of Political Economy.* Darwin, *On the Origin of Species by Means of Natural Selection.*

1861 American Civil War.

1864 International Worker's Association founded in London. Marx becomes the General Council's Corresponding Secretary for Germany.

1867 *Capital: A Critique of Political Economy, Volume 1.* Disraeli extends male suffrage in Britain.

1871 Paris Commune. *The Civil War in France.*

1872 Nietzsche, *Birth of Tragedy.*

1875 German workers' parties unite at Gotha conference to form the Socialist Workers' Party. *Critique of the Gotha Programme.*

1876 Victoria crowned Empress of India. Dissolution of the International.

1878 Anti-Socialist Law in Germany.

1881 December, death of wife, Jenny.

1883 January, death of daughter, Jenny. 14 March, Marx dies in London. He is buried in Highgate Cemetery.

1885 *Capital, Volume 2.*

1888 English edition of *Capital, Volume 1.*

1894 *Capital, Volume 3.*

1895 Death of Engels.

1905–10 *Theories of Surplus Value.*

1927 *Marx-Engels Collected Edition* begins to appear.

1932 First publication of Marx's early manuscripts.

1938 First publication of *Grundrisse.*

SUGGESTIONS FOR FURTHER READING

Marx

The whole of the 50-volume *Marx-Engels Collected Works* is in the process of being made available online in English at the Marx and Engels Internet Archive at: *www.marxists.org/archive/marx/index.htm*

Marx and Engels, *The Communist Manifesto*, appeared in several new editions in 1998 to coincide with the 150th anniversary of its first publication: Oxford World's Classics, Signet Classics and Verso. The Verso edition has an introduction by the British Marxist historian, Eric Hobsbawm.

The best general selection of Marx's writings is David McLellan (ed.), *Karl Marx: Selected Writings*, 2nd edition, Oxford University Press, Oxford, 2000.

Biography

Werner Blumerberg, *Karl Marx* (1962), Verso, London and New York, 2000

David McLellan, *Karl Marx: His Life and Thought* (1973), Macmillan, London, 1987

Franz Mehring's classic 1918 biography is available online at: *www.marxists.org/archive/mehring/1918/marx/*

Francis Wheen, *Karl Marx*, Fourth Estate, London, 2000

General

Tom Bottomore (ed.), *A Dictionary of Marxist Thought* (1983), 2nd edition, Blackwell, Oxford, 1992

Ernst Fischer, *How to Read Karl Marx*, Monthly Review Press, New York, 1996

Leszek Kolakowski, *Main Currents of Marxism, Volume 1: The Founders*, Oxford University Press, Oxford, 1981

Ernest Mandel, *The Formation of the Economic Thought of Karl Marx: 1843 to Capital*, Monthly Review Press, New York, 1971

S. S. Prawer, *Karl Marx and World Literature*, Oxford University Press, Oxford, 1976

Philosophy

C. J. Arthur, *Dialectics of Labour: Marx and His Relation to Hegel*, Blackwell, Oxford, 1986

Étienne Balibar, *The Philosophy of Marx*, Verso, London and New York, 1995

Carol C. Gould, *Marx's Social Ontology*, MIT Press, Cambridge MA, 1978

Karl Korsch, *Marxism and Philosophy* (1923), available online at: *www.marxists.org/archive/korsch/1923/marxism-philosophy.htm*

Herbert Marcuse, 'The Foundations of Historical Materialism' (1932), in *From Luther to Popper: Studies in Critical Philosophy*, Verso, London, 1988

Istvan Meszaros, *Marx's Theory of Alienation* (1970), Merlin Press, London, 1986

Bertell Ollman, *Alienation*, 2nd edition (1977), Cambridge University Press, Cambridge, 1996

Alfred Schmidt, *The Concept of Nature in Marx*, New Left Books, London, 1971

History

G. A. Cohen, *Karl Marx's Theory of History: A Defence* (1978), revised edition, Oxford University Press, Oxford, 2000

Umberto Melotti, *Marx and the Third World*, Macmillan, London, 1982

Alfred Schmidt, *History and Structure* (1971), MIT Press, Cambridge MA and London, 1983

Politics

Hal Draper, *Karl Marx's Theory of Revolution*, 4 volumes, Monthly Review Press, New York, 1977ff.

R. N. Hunt, *The Political Ideas of Marx and Engels*, 2 Volumes, University of Pittsburg Press, Pittsburg, 1974

Ralph Miliband, *Marxism and Politics* (1977), Merlin Press, London, 2004

Leo Panitch and Colin Leys (eds.), *Socialist Register 1998. The Communist Manifesto Now*, Merlin Press, London, 1998

Capital and the Critique of Political Economy

Anthony Brewer, *A Guide to Marx's Capital*, Cambridge University Press, Cambridge, 1984

Harry Cleaver, *Reading Capital Politically* (1979), 2nd edition, AK Press, 1999

Ben Fine, *Marx's Capital*, 3rd edition, Macmillan, London, 1989

INDEX